60 Days for 60 Years

Remember the past to build the future

Editor: Rabbi Andrew Shaw

YOUNG UNITED SYNAGOGUE

Tribe is part of the United Synagogue Community Development Group

community
development
united synagogue

In memory of the six million

First Published in Great Britain 2005 by Tribe,
Young United Synagogue
Adler House
735 High Road
London, N12 0US
Charity Number: 242552
Enquiries: info@tribeuk.com
Website: www.tribeuk.com

ISBN 0-9549397-0-0

Editorial team – Rabbi Andrew Shaw, David Kaplan, Rabbi Aubrey
Hersh, Chayali Fehler, Ian Myers

Designed by Ethical Communications, London

Printed and bound in Great Britain by Kellmatt, Middlesex

Preface

The 60 Days for 60 Years Project
Rabbi Andrew Shaw

60 years ago six million of our people were murdered in the darkest period of our history.

In the world today there is a time for everything under the sun: a time to be silent and a time to speak, a time to refrain and a time to learn, a time to remember and a time to forget. Now is the time to remember, to learn and to speak. Be involved for the sake of the past, the present and the future.

In 1985, Rabbi Shapira attended the commemoration of *Theresienstadt* concentration camp, forty years after its liberation. Two thoughts struck him. First, could anything positive be taken from such a tragedy? The second thought was more worrying. He, an orphan of the Holocaust, could personally remember the dark years of 1939 – 1945, but what about his children and their children. How would they remember?

He returned to Israel and contacted Yad Vashem. They supplied the names of thirty children who died in the Holocaust. He gave these names to thirty children in his home city of Netanya and asked each of them to learn in memory of one Holocaust victim.

It was this idea that inspired me to embark on the project 'Fifty Days for Fifty Years' when working for the Union of Jewish Students in 1995. Five thousand Jewish students across the United Kingdom received the name of a victim of student age and were asked to learn in their memory for fifty days: a chance to remember the past to build the future.

Along with the name, students also received a pocket book containing fifty questions and ideas about various aspects of Judaism chosen by students from across the country. The answers were provided by scholars, rabbis and professors from around the world.

Ten years have now passed since that project. However the idea remains as alive and relevant today as it was back in 1995. Then we remembered five thousand, ten years on we hope to remember hundreds of thousands.

This new book contains sixty thought-provoking questions, ideas, stories and articles which provide an entry point to issues crucial to our religion and people. The articles reflect the author's own personal viewpoint. It is up to you the reader to take the study further, to find out what it means to be a Jew today, a journey which I hope this book will facilitate.

This book gives a daily focus for any study that will be embarked upon. For those who wish to take their studying further, we have also included as a footnote to each day's article a selection of Psalms and Mishnah.

As you begin the sixty days of commemoration, consider the following. There are Jews reading this who are teenagers, there are Jews reading this who are in their seventies and eighties. There are Jews reading this in English, there are Jews reading this in Russian, Hebrew and Spanish. There are Jews reading this in America, there are Jews reading this in South Africa, Denmark and Germany.

Sixty years ago a nation had risen up to gather us together to destroy us. Sixty years on we are gathering together to learn in memory of those who were murdered and to learn for our future.

The sixty days should be used as a time of commemoration for the person in whose memory you are learning and for the town in which they lived: a person who had similar dreams, hopes, aspirations, until their life was tragically cut short. Let us reclaim their lives from the Holocaust, let us as Chief Rabbi Sacks says "give them a living memorial".

For sixty days I urge you to get involved. Not just for a Jewish life that never had the chance, but also for us, Jews in 2005 who are the guardians of our three thousand year old heritage.

Be a part of one of the most ambitious and inspiring ideas ever attempted in the Jewish world. We all have a chance in the next two months to remember a past that no longer is, and in those same two months we have a chance to help build the future. The Jewish future, our future.

Rabbi Andrew Shaw
January 2005
Shevat 5765

Contents

Acknowledgements

For a project of such magnitude, there are so many people to thank. The compilation of this book and the running of the project have taken months of work from so many quarters. It is impossible to thank every person who has contributed to making 60 Days for 60 Years a reality; however the following deserve special mention.

- Rabbi Shapira from Netanya, whose ideas 20 years ago were the catalyst for this project.
- Rabbi Hool who gave me the inspiration for the Fifty Days project in 1994.
- Chief Rabbi Dr Jonathan Sacks who has been a friend and strong supporter from the start of the original project ten years ago whose support continues to this day.
- Syma Weinberg for all her time and effort on our behalf.
- David Kaplan for his support and being the rock on which the whole project has been built.
- Rabbi Hersh for giving up so many nights to be an invaluable help with editing the essays – we couldn't have done it without him.
- Yossi Fachler for believing in the project from the start and making it 'huge'.
- My wife Gila, helping out night after night despite being eight months pregnant.
- Jeremy Jacobs for his support and confidence.
- Sheryl Kaplan for her support and sustenance.
- Richard Marcus for all his hours of help late into the night.
- Marc (Moishele) Levene for coordinating the marketing campaign, the late nights and everything else.
- The rest of the team at Tribe: Debbie, Kerry and Michelle for all their help and advice.
- Dayan Abraham for his advice and guidance.
- Gabby Kosky for typing up many of the articles.
- Esther Jacobs for her patience and her proof reading.
- Rabbi Laitner for his editing skills and sense of humour.

- Rabbi Zneimer for his leadership and backing.
- Leonie Lewis and the team at the Community Development Group of the United Synagogue.
- Rabbi Waxman and the Orthodox Union for partnering us in the project.
- Yad Vashem in Israel and the UK for their support and advice.
- All our donors and supporters for their help in making this project possible.
- Ian Myers and Fiona Palmer from Ethical Communications and Mandy and Johnny Mitchell for all their help with design, production and creative input.
- Simon Maurer and the team at Inspire for their contribution to web-media.
- Ivor Rosenthal and the staff at Kellmatt for printing and distribution.
- And finally, the wonderful director of the project Chayali Fehler whose determination and perseverance has turned the dream into reality.

Rabbi Andrew Shaw
January 2005
Shevat 5765

Letters of Support

office of the
CHIEF RABBI

60 Days for 60 Years is a wonderfully imaginative project, and behind it lies a set of profound Jewish ideas.

The first is remembering for life: the idea that we take the tragedies of Jewish history and turn them into lessons for the future. What the victims of the *Shoah* died for, we commit ourselves to live for. We cannot bring the dead back to life, but we can bring their memory back to life and ensure that they are not forgotten – and that we undertake in our lives to do what they were so cruelly prevented from doing.

The second is learning as a bond between the living and the dead. The words of Torah are beyond time, and through them we are connected with all previous generations of Jews. Learning in the name of one of the victims of the *Shoah* symbolically rewrites their letter into the Torah scroll of the Jewish people.

The third is the act of rededication. One third of our people died in the *Shoah*, but the Jewish people as a whole refused to die. A mere three years after the *Shoah* it created the greatest single collective affirmation of Jewish life in two thousand years: the State of Israel. Every Jew today carries the legacy of the past and its hopes for the future. The most important thing we can possibly do is to ensure that Judaism and the Jewish people face the future with confidence and commitment. That is our gift to the past – and its challenge to us.

So: congratulations to all those who have brought this project to fruition – and thanks to you for taking part. May your sixty days of study turn the memory of one of the victims of the *Shoah* into a blessing.
With every good wish,

Chief Rabbi Dr Jonathan Sacks
Chief Rabbi of the United Hebrew Congregations of the Commonwealth

The last few years have been extremely exciting for the United Synagogue. We are an organisation that is responsible for the Jewish lives of some 30,000 families in England. Nearly 100,000 people within British-Jewry are touched by the United Synagogue. We take our responsibilities seriously and by launching Tribe – the Young United Synagogue – under the inspired direction of Rabbi Andrew Shaw and David Kaplan we are making a statement about the importance of our long term future. Tribe is all about connecting our young people to vibrant Jewish life and Torah values.

This project, 60 Days for 60 Years, the brainchild of Rabbi Shaw, is a fantastic example of how a great educational programme rooted in Torah can have an impact well beyond what was originally envisaged. The idea of giving Jews, young and old, the opportunity to study Torah each day for 60 days and commemorate those who died *al kiddush Hashem* in the Holocaust, is a simple but profoundly effective one. The fact that it has been embraced by so many both in the United Kingdom and beyond is testimony to the power of the concept.

The United Synagogue is proud of Tribe and of this project. We firmly believe that it will raise the awareness of Jews the world over, of the beauty and insight of Torah and our tradition. Our sages say, "Hafuch bah ve hafuch bah ki kula bah – Turn it over and turn it over again, because you will find everything there." Through 60 Days for 60 Years, we are delighted to be giving that opportunity to so many.

Rabbi Saul Zneimer
Chief Executive
The United Synagogue

I am especially gratified by this work and by this project. Gratified because I have long been waiting for a work which addresses the primary issues of faith and belief arising from the horrible experience of the Holocaust. The Holocaust has occasioned a broad literature, ranging from detailed historical descriptions and elaborate historical theories to distorted and forced theological positions. What has been lacking has been a traditional approach to the questions of faith prompted by the evil of the Holocaust and an adequate portrayal of the religious and spiritual response of the victims of the Holocaust to their unspeakable personal dilemmas.

I have personally long taken the position that for a person of deep religious faith there is value in studying the events and background of the Holocaust. Not just to remember evil, and not only to suffer along with the agony experienced by our brothers and sisters who were victims, but to be inspired by the demonstrations of courage, heroism and religious observance that occurred during those very dark years. Furthermore, I have always yearned for Holocaust studies to pay more attention to pre-Holocaust European Jewry, its communities, institutions, and its people. What we have lost most of all, and this is especially apparent as time moves on, is the deep religiosity and creative spiritual strength of all that was destroyed by Hitler and his hordes. We lost entire communities with centuries of exemplary history; institutions of learning and chesed that remain unparalleled in our annals; and individuals whose scholarship and natural piety have not yet been recreated.

This project, and this book, begin to address these serious gaps in a comprehensive and authentic manner. There are, thankfully, other similar projects currently being planned to restore to the centre stage of Holocaust study, the role played by the vast majority of the six million who were proud of their Jewish heritage, Jewish practices and profound Jewish beliefs. Perhaps once and for all the myth of the secularity and ordinariness of the victims of the Holocaust will be dispelled and we will look at the six million not as victims but as heroes. Every step toward that goal is to be valued and the project of "60 Days for 60 Years" takes more than one step in that direction.

I am honoured to have been asked to provide words of introduction to this programme and I commend it highly to all my friends and acquaintances and recommend it to the entire Jewish community.

Respectfully,
Rabbi Dr Tzvi Hersh Weinreb
Executive Vice President
Union of Orthodox Jewish Congregations of America

Sixty years after the darkest period in our nation's long history, we must confront a terrible truth. Despite the lessons that should have been learned from the Holocaust, the phenomenon of anti-Semitism remains widespread around the world.

The Jewish community in Britain in particular has suffered greatly. Over the past year the Community Security Trust has recorded the highest ever number of anti-Semitic incidents. Recalling terrible scenes of the past, synagogues have been burned, rabbis abused in the streets, children attacked on their way to school – all because these people and institutions either are Jewish or symbolise our continued Jewish existence.

Our response to this attempt to drive us back into the dark past must be to redouble our efforts to build a better future. The greatest credit to those who lost their lives in the Holocaust is the way that we live our lives, and the extent to which we renew our commitment to our Jewish values and heritage.

This wonderful initiative is an affirmation of hope for the future, and our guarantee that the victims of the Holocaust will not be forgotten.

Gerald M Ronson
Chairman
Community Security Trust

The drive to ask questions is a powerful one, especially when confronted by profound issues. It is perhaps unsurprising therefore that ten years ago it was amongst students that this book was first conceived. It's no secret that Jews like to ask questions, and this is especially true for Jewish students.

As an organisation that understands just how important it is to be able to respond to questions with meaningful answers, Jewish Chaplaincy is proud to be supporting the 60 Days for 60 Years project.

The future of our community rests with its youth and so it is a great pleasure to work with Tribe in support of this and many other initiatives.

With all best wishes

Ian Myers
Chairman
National Jewish Chaplaincy Board

In 1995 the Union of Jewish Students ran a project to mark the fiftieth anniversary of the end of the Holocaust. A pocket book was produced entitled 'Fifty Days for Fifty Years,' which contained fifty questions about contemporary Jewish life answered by rabbis and scholars across the Jewish world. Ten years on from the publication of this book, and sixty years on from the end of the Holocaust, the book has been recreated and renamed '60 Days for 60 Years'.

Avraham Infeld, the President of Hillel International in the United States, asks the question "What is Jewish education?" He answers it claiming that, "It is asking 'How do I link the individual Jew to the collective memory of the Jewish people?'" But what is the collective memory of the Jewish people? What are the defining moments in the recent history of the Jewish people which have formed our collective memory? I would argue that two memories stand out – one catastrophic and one joyous – yet both as monumental as each other.

This year we will commemorate sixty years since the end of the Holocaust. During the darkest period of our history, when the Nazis sought the systematic extermination of the Jewish people, over six million Jews lost their lives simply because they were Jewish.

Out of the ashes of the Holocaust rose a second collective memory of the Jewish people. The birth of the State of Israel on May 14th 1948 marked the culmination of thousands of years of yearning and exile for the Jewish people. At long last the Jewish people had a land they could call their own; a place where they could be free from fear. The Biblical promise had become a modern reality.

The challenge of UJS today is to ensure that Jewish students maintain and strengthen their links to Judaism and the collective memory of the Jewish people. The role and obligation of each generation of the Jewish people is to inspire the next, engaging them in their Judaism and ensuring the continued love for the religion to which they belong. It is our challenge to ignite the spark of Judaism within each and every Jew so that they feel they belong to a wider community. It is our responsibility never to forget the sacrifice of all those killed in the Holocaust.

By being proud to be a Jew, you can ensure that the spark of Judaism which the Nazis attempted to extinguish in our parents and grandparents' generations continues to burn brighter than ever before in ours. In doing so we can remember the past in order to build a better future.

Daniel Sacker
UJS Chairperson 2004-05

✡UJIA

Memory has been essential to Jewish survival. Our ability to remember our roots, our traditions, our stories and rituals has enabled us to thrive as a distinct people while other great civilizations have disappeared. Emil Fakenheim, a Holocaust survivor and Jewish thinker of the 20th century, proposed a new commandment in addition to the traditional 613. His 614th commandment was "to survive". But survival for its own sake is not enough. Whilst marking the past, we must take actions to secure a Jewish future – through education and commitment to our values and our heritage.

As a child of Holocaust survivors, I know how important it is for memories to be etched deeply into one's own being, in order to ensure Jewish survival. My late father Leo Leon taught me to see each day as a gift. Through 60 Days for 60 Years, thousands of us will be taking time out each day to learn. We will not only sanctify those whose lives were lost in the Holocaust, we will affirm our most valuable of Jewish traditions.

As a leading supporter of the people of Israel and young Jewish people in the UK, the UJIA is committed to laying the foundation for a vibrant community of the future. By investing in our children's Jewish identity, by exposing them to exciting Jewish activities, such as those run by Tribe, by giving them rich and meaningful experiences in Israel, and by developing the best possible Jewish educators to inspire them, we can ensure that there will be a Jewish future in the UK. The UJIA is proud to invest in Tribe, and my congratulations go to all who are part of this exciting programme. May every day of learning, and of remembering the past, enhance our commitment to building our Jewish future.

Benjamin Leon
Chief Executive, United Jewish Israel Appeal

Remember the Past
to Build the Future

Continuity From the Ashes

Sir Martin Gilbert
Renowned holocaust historian and author

Sixty years ago the Second World War was in its final stages. Although victory over Hitler was by then a certainty, the Jews of Europe were still suffering. Hundreds of thousands of those who had survived ghettos, deportations and concentration camps – including Auschwitz – were on the move, driven by their captors across Germany in death marches in which tens of thousands died. But liberation was in sight. The Allied armies – British, American, Soviet and French – were about to drive deep into the German heartland.

Jewish soldiers from British Mandate Palestine, who were among the 90,000 Jewish volunteers from the Land of Israel who fought on land, sea and air, were fighting alongside the other armies in Italy, playing their part in the defeat of the German war machine.

With the defeat of Hitler came liberation. The surviving Jews were frail and frightened, and did not know where they could go to rebuild their lives. The places they had lived in before the war, in particular Poland, were hostile to those who returned. The Displaced Persons camps, some located in the very concentration camps in which they had been liberated, were only a temporary haven. Yet even there, education flourished and the Jewish spirit was renewed.

The soldiers of the Jewish Brigade, who but a short time earlier were fighting the German war machine, emerged as helpers and facilitators of the long, arduous but uplifting 'Bricha', the movement of a hundred thousand survivors across the mountains from Austria into Italy, and on by ship to Palestine. Many were intercepted by British warships and interned behind barbed wire in Cyprus. But with the establishment of the State of Israel in 1948, they were taken to the new homeland, where they fought from the first days for its survival against the attacks of five separate Arab armies.

Other survivors, liberated in Theresienstadt in the last week of the war, were flown to Britain in Royal Air Force bombers, to begin a new life in a strange but welcoming land. Today, these young men and women are rightly proud of what their children, and now their grandchildren, are contributing to British life.

The Jewish imperative, "Choose life", has always been a redeeming and enhancing feature of Jewish communities everywhere, as has "Seek justice and pursue it". Thus from the depths of despair sixty years ago, new light and a renewed faith have brought strength and continuity.

Remembering the People Behind the Names

Avner Shalev
Chairman of the Yad Vashem Directorate

"I should like someone to remember that there once lived a person named David Berger…"

These words were written by a young Jewish man, from the Polish town of Przemysl. When war broke out in 1939, David Berger fled the approaching German army towards Vilna. During his stay in the city, David corresponded with his girlfriend Else, who had emigrated to Palestine in 1938. In one postcard, David said his farewells, aware that he would not survive. He was shot in Vilna in July 1941, at the age of twenty-two.

The project to collect the names of Holocaust victims was inspired by the legacy of David Berger and other Jews who left similar requests. Following the terrible years of the Holocaust, the Jewish people began to search for a way to salvage the memory of those who perished. Each person represented an unending potential chain of creation, lost to humanity. Unable to express the complete life story of each victim – each world that was extinguished – Yad Vashem sought to convey its loss through gathering and commemorating the one symbol of identity the victims left behind: their names.

From the moment a person is born, their name becomes their identity. The mere mention of someone's name invokes memories of their personality, character and achievements. Commemorating names is a unique form of memory in Jewish history, and particular to the Holocaust. Most of the victims have no official resting place or tombstone to testify they once lived. Tens of thousands of families were totally obliterated, without a single survivor to remember them or be named after them. As we document the victims' names and the lives that were lost, private memorials have been turned into public commemoration for the Jewish people and all humanity.

Contrary to popular conception, in most cases the Germans did not create orderly lists of names of those they murdered. In many cases, they ignored their names and replaced them with numbers, in an effort to annihilate not just the people themselves, but also their identities. Redeeming their names has always depended mainly on those who remember or knew them. Since its establishment, Yad Vashem has encouraged surviving relatives and friends to fill out Pages of Testimony – special forms for Holocaust victims containing biographical details such as date of birth, nickname, profession, place of residence prior to the war, and more – which are then stored for perpetuity in Yad Vashem's Hall of Names. These Pages represent our effort to touch the world of every Jew lost in the Holocaust, to rebuild their individual identities, and to commemorate their lives.

The Central Database of Holocaust Victims' names currently includes some three million names, including two million from Pages of Testimony and another million from archives and other sources. In order to preserve their memory and redeem as many names as possible from all over the world, Yad Vashem has recently uploaded the Database to its website (www.yadvashem.org). I encourage all students of Judaism who are taking part in this unique project, 60 Days for 60 Years to search the site and learn more about the lives of the individuals whose memories they are commemorating. I also urge you all to join our vital mission of collecting names not yet recorded in our Database. You may assist survivors in your families and communities to fill out Pages of Testimony, or add missing details directly online. These names are part of our common history and national heritage: help us to preserve them in our collective memory for generations to come.

One Person, One Name

Rabbi Yisrael Meir Lau
Former Chief Rabbi of Israel

It wasn't until I came to the American Society for Yad Vashem's annual dinner that I finally realised how to convey the horror of the Holocaust to the next generation.

What was the reason survivors kept quiet for decades following the war? It was because nobody could understand six million deaths. It was too big a number to comprehend.

At eight years old I was the youngest survivor of Buchenwald. When I was ten years old I picked up *The Diary of Anne Frank*. I wanted to see what everybody was talking about. I was astonished. That's all? The whole book is not to be compared to one day in Buchenwald. Where is the concentration camp, the torture, the killings? I couldn't understand why people were so excited about this book.

When I got older, I realised that the book's success lay in the fact that it didn't speak about millions. It was one person's story. With one human being you can identify.

For the first time I understood what Yad Vashem means. As it says in Isaiah: "I will give them *yad vashem* – a hand and a name." One hand, one name. If it is single it will convince you. You cannot bear millions of deaths, but one name you can understand.

That was why Anne Frank's diary was so powerful – it was the story of one individual. Anyone can identify with another single human being. And that is why 60 Days for 60 Years is so powerful – we each can identify with one victim and learn in their memory – one person, one name.

Pictures From the Past

The following photos are used with kind permission from the Yad Vashem archives.

1. *Synagogue in Berlin 1912.* By 1938 Jews had been living in Germany for over 1,100 years and their oldest synagogue was 800 years old.

2. *The above synagogue after the Nazis had destroyed it on Kristallnacht 9 November 1938.* In a 24 hour period the Germans burnt almost 200 synagogues. The *Jews* were fined 1 billion Reichsmarks to pay for the damages.

3. *A Jewish couple on their wedding day wearing the yellow star.* From 1933 onwards Jews in Germany were targeted. Jews were banned from cinemas, denied jobs and stripped of citizenship.

4. *Two Jewish pupils being humiliated by their teacher in front of their non-Jewish classmates.* The writing on the blackboard reads: "The Jew is our greatest enemy. Beware of the Jew."

5. *The wall of the Warsaw Ghetto, created in November 1940.* Half a million Jews, (including 30% of the population of Warsaw), were packed into less than 3% of the city's area and all 22 entrances were closed off. Any Jew found outside of the Ghetto would be shot.

6. *Scarce food being shared in the Warsaw Ghetto.* The Jews were forced to live on 180 grams of bread a day; 15% of the minimum daily requirement for survival. By the time that the Ghetto was liquidated, over 100,000 had died of disease and starvation, mostly children and the elderly.

7. *Rabbi Moshe Hagerman being forced to pray in desecrated Tefillin, in front of abused Jews.* For the Nazis, inflicting physical deprivation and hardship wasn't enough. Their goal was de-humanisation.

8. *Jews forced under heavy guard to dig their own graves.*

9. *A Jew being killed by the Einsatzgruppen.* These mobile killing units consisted of SS men and volunteers from the local Ukrainian, Polish and Lithuanian population. During 1941 they murdered approximately 1 million Jews mostly in broad daylight, burying them in mass graves.

10. *Desecrated Torah scrolls.* The fate of the holy books of the Jews mirrored that of their owners: violated, abused and burnt.

11. *Shabbat in the Warsaw Ghetto.* Despite being forced to labour seven days a week, and in defiance of the German ban on public prayer, secret prayer groups gathered throughout Warsaw.

12. *Lighting Chanukah candles in a work camp in Westerbork, Holland.* Despite their suffering, Jews struggled to maintain their traditions.

13. *Liquidation of the Warsaw Ghetto.* "Suddenly four armed Germans materialised in front of us ... And so began our long journey to Majdanek, to Auschwitz. This is how the resistance in the Warsaw Ghetto ended for us."
(Dr Hillel Seidman – Ghetto survivor.)

14. *Train transport arriving in Auschwitz-Birkenau.* In the course of seven weeks, beginning in May of 1944, more than 430,000 Hungarian Jews were sent to Auschwitz.

15. *Jews standing outside the cattle trucks.* In 1944 Jews under 16, the elderly and women accompanying young children were automatically selected to be gassed. Of the people in this photograph, only 2 (Lilli and Herczi Klein) survived.

16. *Israel and Zelig Jacob, transported to Auschwitz from Beregszasz in Hungary in May 1944.* Both were gassed on the day they arrived.

17. *The infamous 'selection' being carried out beside the railway tracks in Auschwitz-Birkenau.* At the top of the photo a line of people are being marched to the gas chambers and crematoria.

"'Men to the left, women to the right.' Eight words spoken quietly, indifferently. Eight short simple words. I did not know that at that place, at that moment, I was parting from my mother and from Tzipora forever."
(Elie Wiesel – Auschwitz survivor.)

18. *An elderly woman taking care of 3 little children - 26 May 1944.* They are walking to the gas chambers.

60 Days for 60 Years

1 Remembering the Past to Build the Future

Chief Rabbi Dr Jonathan Sacks

The Holocaust is a black hole in human history. There was never anything like it before, and if humanity is to be worthy of its existence there will never be anything like it again.

At some time in the spring or early summer of 1941, Hitler issued an order for a "Final Solution of the Jewish Question", a brutal euphemism for the planned, systematic destruction of the Jewish people. Four years later, as the Second World War came to an end, the first soldiers to enter the concentration camps began to realise what had been done, and they did not believe it. Six million human beings, among them one and a half million children, had been shot, gassed, burned or buried alive for no other reason than that they were Jews. Where once there had been community after community of sages and scholars, poets and mystics, intellectuals and visionaries, there was the stench of death. As Jews we mourn, and still today we refuse to be comforted.

The Holocaust raises many questions. In an essay entitled "*Kol Dodi Dofek*", the late Rabbi Yosef Soloveitchik made a profound distinction between two Jewish responses to suffering. There is the metaphysical question, "Why did this happen?" But there is also the *halachic* question, "What then shall I do?" The halachic response invites us to react to tragedy not as objects but as subjects, not as figures of fate but as masters of our destiny. We are not defined by what happens to us but by how we respond.

Judaism has never sought to deny the existence of evil. But equally it has not sought to come to terms with it by explaining it away, mystically or metaphysically. There is, says Rabbi Soloveitchik, a theological answer to "Why did this happen?" But it must always elude us, for we are not God nor can we see events from the perspective of eternity. Halachah summons us not to understand and thus accept the existence of evil, but instead to fight it as partners with God in the process of redemption.

In this mode of Jewish spirituality there is a profound insistence on human dignity often in the face of immense and unfathomable suffering. The halachic response is not naïve. It does not hide from questions, but it is courageous. It says: we must continue to affirm Jewish life even in the absence of answers. In that, there is a faith that defies even the angel of death.

One of the most important halachic responses to tragedy is the act of remembering, *Yizkor*. More than it has history, the Jewish people has memory. There is no word for history in the *Tenach*, and modern Hebrew had to borrow one, *historiah*. But the word *zachor*, remember, occurs no less than 169 times in the Hebrew Bible. The difference between them is this. History is someone else's story. Memory is my story. In history, we recall what happened, so that it becomes part of us and who we are. History is the story of a past that is dead. Memory is the story of a future. We cannot bring the dead to life, but we can keep their memory alive. That is what the Jewish people always did for those who died as martyrs *al kiddush Hashem* (sanctifying God's name). They never forgot them, as we must never forget the victims of the Holocaust.

But there is a specifically Jewish way of remembering. When the word *yizkor* is mentioned in the Torah it refers not to the past but to the present and to renewal. "*V'Yizkor Elokim et Rachel* – God remembered Rachel" and gave her a child, and thus new life. "*V'Yizkor Elokim et Britav* – God remembered His covenant" and began the process of rescuing the Israelites from Egypt. When we remember as Jews we do so for the sake of the future, so that those who died may live on in us.

Commemorating the sixty years that have passed with sixty

days of study, linking individuals with holocaust victims and communities with communities that perished – this is the Jewish way of remembering. Few things could do more to give those who died a living memorial.

At the core of Judaism is an affirmation of life. Unlike other religions we do not venerate death. In Judaism, death defiles. Moses asked the Israelites to "Choose life", and his words still echo today. One third of our people died because they were Jews. The most profound Judaic affirmation we can make is to live because we are Jews; to live as Jews, affirming our faith with courage, our identity with pride, refusing to be traumatised by evil or intimidated by anti-Semitism.

Whenever, through indifference or fear, we drift away from living as Jews, the Holocaust claims yet more belated victims. As one of the contributors to this book reminds us, Hitler's anti-semitism was not accidental. Hitler declared that "conscience is a Jewish invention" and he was right. Nazi Germany was intended to demonstrate the triumph of everything Jews have fought against since the days of *Abraham* and *Sarah*: might as against right, power as against justice, racism as opposed to the respect for human dignity, violence as opposed to the sanctity of human life. Jews have always lived by and for a different set of values, and as a result we have always been called on to have the courage to be different. We need that courage now. It is not too much to say that humanity needs it now.

If each of us in the coming year makes a significant personal gesture to show that Judaism is alive and being lived, there can be no more momentous signal to humanity that evil does not have the final victory, because *Am Yisrael Chai*, the Jewish people lives.

2 The Eternal Message

Chief Rabbi Warren Goldstein

As a result of archaeological finds, we have letters dating back 2,500 years to the time of the destruction of the First Temple. One of these letters consists of a message from a military commander by the name of Hoshea, who was in charge of a garrison of Jewish soldiers, defending the eastern border of the land of Israel. They were under attack by Babylonian soldiers, and the message he sent back to headquarters in Jerusalem read: "Please send the four species." *Succot* was approaching and Hoshea and his men were asking for the four plant species needed to fulfill the mitzvah of *lulav*.

2,500 years later at the beginning of the Yom Kippur War in 1973, an Israeli Defence Force commander by the name of Yehoshua sent a message back to his headquarters in Jerusalem which read: "Please send the four species". In Hebrew, the two messages were exactly the same. Hoshea and Yehoshua had almost the same names, and were asking for the same things, in the same language, and yet, they lived 2,500 years apart. In fact, a Jew of that time could walk into our synagogues and homes today and understand our prayers, our Torah learning and our *mitzvot*.

This amazing manifestation of our endurance through the ages reveals much more than just a profound sense of Jewish continuity and pride in our roots. Being Jewish is not about historical continuity for its own sake. Jewish survival is too costly and painful an exercise to be pursued as a value and end in itself. Our Jewish state is under constant threat and across the world Jews struggle to maintain their identity as Jews. Why continue with the enterprise of the Jewish people? What does it really mean to be Jewish?

The crisis of resurgent anti-semitism has forced us to consider this fundamental question. We can never allow ourselves to be defined by anti-semitism. Some philosophers have sought to do that. Jean-Paul Sartre said: "The Jew is one whom other men consider a Jew. It is the anti-Semite who makes the Jew. It is neither their past, their religion nor their soil that unites the sons of Israel. The sole ties that bind them are the hostility and disdain of the societies which surround them." Sadly, we ourselves often give credence to these offensive words. But we must disprove them. We must be proud of our Jewish identity, know what it means to be Jewish, why we want to be Jewish and why we need the land of Israel. We dare not allow ourselves to be defined in terms of those who hate us. We have to have a positive sense of self-identity. This means redefining for ourselves why we want the State of Israel and what it means to be a Jew.

And what does it mean to be a Jew? Why should we continue as a people? The answer to that question lies at the foot of *Mount Sinai*, where we all stood a mere 130 generations ago, and accepted God's Torah and His mission for our people and the world. What it means to be a Jew is that our ancestors stood at Mount Sinai, three thousand three hundred years ago, when God gave us His law, His morals, His ethics, His instructions and His principles. He taught us how to lead our personal lives, how to build a country, how to lead our lives as private citizens, and how to lead our lives as part of a national entity. It is worthwhile to continue as the Jewish people because we were given a mission by God at Mount Sinai 3,300 years ago. Our Divine mission summons and commands us to continue.

And the Torah is more relevant now than ever before. It tells us what God proposes for the world and for our individual lives. We have something very precious which all of mankind craves, and that is a connection to something greater than ourselves. In a rootless world we are anchored in a tradition which spans more than three millennia and endures. We have a sense of belonging. We have God's direction for our lives. We have a document which contains the words and thoughts of God concerning how we should conduct our lives. The Torah tells us what God proposes for the world and for our individual lives.

The Torah remains relevant to us today, at the beginning of the new millennium, because it is the blueprint of the world. When God created the world, our Sages teach us, He used the Torah as the basis for creation. Our Sages are telling us that our Torah is in sync with the world and its people. Externals may change, but in essence people remain the same, whether they use smoke signals to communicate or e-mail. The Torah tells us how God wants us and our society to function, and is eternally relevant. The more connected we are to the Torah, the more connected we are to His truth about ourselves and our lives.

The Torah has relevant and real solutions to problems that we as people have to face. Rabbi Moshe Feinstein, one of our greatest rabbinic authorities in recent times, dealt with the most complex problems that a modern society has to offer and solved them using the principles of the Torah. Rabbi Feinstein came to the United States from Eastern Europe before World War Two. People from across America and the world brought questions to him. He lived through a time of arguably unprecedented technological and economic growth in the most advanced country in history. The questions he faced ranged from those concerning heart transplants, artificial insemination and other medical ethics issues, to business matters, such as the *halachic* significance of a company's limited liability. He even addressed the issue of carrying out the death penalty in the USA, in a letter written to President Ronald Reagan. Difficult ethical questions about marital problems, and how to repent after having stolen and defrauded, were all answered by Rabbi Feinstein. A bewildering array of problems were brought to him and he solved them using the principles of *Talmudic* law that God has given us. The answers were, of course, not his but God's.

Our continuity is built on our faith in our Divine mission and on our connection to the Creator and Sustainer of the Universe and His Torah.

3 Be Happy

Dr Abraham Twerski

From the scientific viewpoint, man is *Homo Sapiens*, or a gorilla with intellect. The distinctive feature of man therefore, is his mind. If a sub-human form of life could somehow be made more intelligent, it would no longer be sub-human but rather human. This kind of thinking, viewed from another angle, has resulted in advocacy of infanticide for children who are mentally defective.

For us however, that which distinguishes man from lower forms in life, is spirituality. Spirituality is not a scientific concept, and has nothing to do with intellect nor with the so-called 'higher' mental functions. It is not the 'How' of life, it is the 'Why'.

Lower forms of life are characterised by two instinctual drives: self-preservation and self-gratification. Animals will instinctively gravitate toward pleasure and away from pain and for them, there is nothing that is more obvious or important than these self-directed drives. Which means that the human being who considers himself superior to say, a cow, merely because he can operate a computer and enjoy a television drama is in a sense actually superior only *quantitatively*, because he has not risen above his animalistic drives.

We might think therefore, that all altruistic or philanthropic deeds are *qualitatively* different and must be truly human, since they are directed toward someone other than oneself. However, just a bit of analysis will reveal that noble as these deeds may be, unless they are performed in compliance with the dictates of a Supreme Being, that actually they emanate from internal drives, the frustration of which would result in feelings of distress; I am charitable because it hurts *me* to see someone in hunger or out in the cold. Hence, these outwardly-directed acts are ultimately still self-gratifying, even if others are helped in the process. It is only when one acts at the behest of a supra-human being that one transcends the animal self and becomes uniquely human.

The real test of the animal/human divide is man's response to suffering. Obviously, self-gratification and suffering are opposites since gratification requires the elimination of suffering. Consequently, if self-gratification is the goal of life, there can be no fulfillment in suffering; only the person who lives life for a higher objective, can find meaning, purpose and even joy in suffering.

Chassidic writings abound with this idea. The *Baal Shem Tov* taught that the awareness of the fact that one has within himself a *neshamah*, a Divine soul which is part of the Almighty, and that one has a unique and specific mission on earth, should so overshadow any suffering, that one should always be in a state of simcha – joy. He expounded his teachings of simcha to Jews living under conditions of extreme poverty and oppression.

I too was brought up with this attitude. "Lebedig, kinderlach, lebedig!" ("Lively, my children, be lively!") was Father's most frequent admonition. Father exuded a spirit of joy with his very presence. Even his memory is comforting and refreshing and it is interesting that anyone speaking of him today invariably smiles.

One day I walked into a patient's room, and after chatting with the patient for a few minutes, the latter said "You know, Rabbi, your father was here yesterday. I had been in terrible pain all day, and nothing the doctors had given me for pain was working. Then your father walked in, and as if by magic, the pain was gone." I left that room knowing that this was an act I could not possibly follow.

Interestingly, there is one beautiful photograph we have of Father, in which he has a very stern expression. Mother swears that this must have been trick photography, because in over fifty years of marriage, she had never seen him with a stern expression. It was a trick all right, but the trick was not in the photography. Rather, it was father's skill in never letting this sternness be communicated.

Father's sternness was essential, for otherwise we would have grown up to be spoiled adults as well as spoiled children. However, just as some vital ingredients in a dish are never tasted as such, but make their presence felt by their effects on the other ingredients, so father's sternness was there, but never identifiable.

Father's personality and demeanour represented to me what Chassidic Jewishness was all about: a pervasive, persistent, and contagious attitude of simcha which was not at all incompatible with some of the harsh realities. In fact, it was precisely when spirits were low that the revitalising charge was heard: "Lebedig, kinderlach, lebedig!" Because Chassidut teaches that simcha can always be achieved.

Indeed the Torah itself, gives as a reason for exile: "Because you have not served God out of a sense of joy."[1] The penalty would seem to be out of all proportion to the crime. The answer is that if I would realise what purpose every moment of my life serves, I would be suffused with an absolute sense of joy. A lack of simcha betrays a lack of conviction in the usefulness of my existence.

But how do I maintain joy? There is far too much suffering in the world. Too much disease, too many accidents, too many so-called 'acts of fate' that cause misery and grief, for which science has failed to provide answers, and which cause wise philosophers to shrug their shoulders.

A follower of the great Chassidic master, the Maggid of Mezeritch, once posed this question to him. "How can the Torah make such a superhuman demand of a person?"

The Maggid referred the man to *Rebbe* Zusia. Whereas all the Maggid's disciples were great scholars, Rebbe Zusia took great pains to keep his scholarship well-concealed. He would do his learning secretly, and never permitted anyone to observe him studying Torah. Incidentally, Rebbe Zusia was the victim of several very painful diseases and his suffering was much aggravated by his extreme poverty.

When the man approached Rebbe Zusia with his question, the latter told him that there had certainly been some mistake,

"Everyone knows I am ignorant of learning," he said. "I know nothing about the *Talmud*. The Maggid must have directed you to someone else."

The man insisted that he had not been mistaken, and was adamant in posing the question to him, which he eventually did. "You see," said Rebbe Zusia, "that just proves that you are mistaken. How could I be expected to explain how one can be grateful for bad things that occur, when I have *never had the experience of anything bad happening to me*?"

The man looked at Rebbe Zusia, who was weak with hunger, racked with pain, and clad in tattered clothes, and understood the answer to his question.

It is widely assumed that simcha is incompatible with suffering. Chassidut reconciled the two. A child who truly knows how intensely his father loves him, and has the intelligence and trust to understand that his father's intentions are solely and exclusively for the child's welfare, would always be grateful for what his father does to him as well as for him, even if he experiences this as distressing and painful.

Just as a sense of purposelessness is the nadir of despair, so is an awareness of purpose the pinnacle of joy. Everything is for a reason, everything is for a purpose. The woman who suffers the pangs of labour may indeed cry out with pain, but the pain is mitigated by her knowledge that she is gaining a child. The anticipation of the ultimate joy of raising a child enables her to joyfully exclaim, "Mazal Tov!" even while the pain-induced tears roll down her cheeks.

Joy is the key to living life fulfilled, it is the key to real happiness.

Notes:
  1. Deuteronomy 28:47

4 Shabbat: A Taste of the World to Come

Dr Akiva Tatz

Shabbat is central to Torah and Jewish living. The week begins and ends with Shabbat — an inspired beginning, a week of work and an inspired end to the week. From the holy to the ordinary to the holy again.

What is the message of this weekly cycle? What energies are being manifest in it that we should be using, riding? Why do we need a Shabbat every week whereas other festivals occur only yearly? There must be a most essential lesson for the *neshamah* in Shabbat which necessitates such close repetition.

There are many ideas in Shabbat, but perhaps the most basic is that it represents an end-point, the purpose of a process. The week is a period of working, building; Shabbat is the cessation of that building, which brings home the significance and sense of achievement that building has generated. It is not simply rest, inactivity. It is the celebration of the work which has been completed. Whenever the Torah mentioned Shabbat it first mentions six days of work — the idea is that Shabbat occurs only after, because of, the work.

A process must have an end-point to give it meaning. If work never achieves a result, the work is foolish. If an inventor builds a machine which maintains itself fully — fuels itself, oils itself, cleans itself — that is clever; provided that the machine produces something useful. A machine whose only output is its own maintenance would be ridiculous.

The result justifies the work, the end-point justifies the process. The pleasure of the freedom and relaxation which accompany an end-point are the direct results of the satisfaction of knowing that the job has to be done. That is the real happiness, the happiness of achievement. Shabbat is wonderful if a person has a week's work to show for that week – then the relaxation is rich and full.

Shabbat is described as *"me'eyn olam ha'ba"* – a small degree of the experience of the next world. There is an idea that all spiritual realities have at least one tangible counterpart in the world so that we can experience them: it would be too difficult to relate to the abstract if we could never have any direct experience of it. Sleep is a sixtieth of the death experience; a dream is a sixtieth of prophecy. Shabbat is a sixtieth of the experience of the next world.

Why specifically a sixtieth? What is unique about the proportion of one in sixty? One who has a sensitive ear will hear something very beautiful here. One in sixty is that proportion which is on the borderline of perception: in the laws of *kashrut* there is a general rule that forbidden mixtures of foods are in fact forbidden only if the admixture of the prohibited component comprises more than one part in sixty. If a drop of milk accidentally spills into a meat dish that dish would not be forbidden if less than one part in sixty were milk – the milk cannot be tasted in such dilution. The *halachic* borderline is set at that point where taste can be discerned.

The beautiful hint here is that Shabbat is one sixtieth of the intensity of *olam ha'ba* – it is on the borderline of taste: if one lives Shabbat correctly one tastes the next world. If not, one will not taste it at all.

How is the higher taste experienced? By desisting from work. Not work in the sense of exertion, that is a serious misconception of Shabbat. What is halted on Shabbat is *melacha* – creative activity. Thirty-nine specific creative actions were needed to build the *Mishkan* in the desert; these mystically parallel the activities God performed to create the Universe – the Mishkan is a microcosm, a model of the Universe. God rested from His creation, we rest from parallel creative actions. The week is built by engaging in those actions constructively, Shabbat is built by desisting from those very actions. The Mishkan represented the dimension of holiness in space, Shabbat is the dimension of holiness in time.

Shabbat rest is an opportunity for introspection. What have I achieved this week? How am I better, more aware, more sensitive? Where do I need to develop in particular? Stocktaking; facing up to oneself honestly. This itself is a faint reflection of the external facing up to oneself which is of the essence of the next world. The meditation of Shabbat is the meditation of being, not becoming. But from that awareness the next week's 'becoming' is generated. Shabbat ends with *havdalah*, the ceremony of 'distinguishing', the holy from the mundane. A profound lesson can be learned from havdalah which is part of the theme we have been studying.

Shabbat exits, the week begins. There is a natural sense of let down, holiness has left, the lower state is experienced. This is why we smell spices at havdalah – to revive the wilting soul. But a deep secret is revealed here: we take wine for havdalah! Wine is used when elevation occurs, as we have noted already. What is the meaning of this paradox?

The idea is as follows. Certainly the week begins with the sadness of sensing Shabbat fade. The relinquishing of holiness is palpable. We smell spices. But the week's beginning means a new opportunity to build, to elevate our present status towards another Shabbat which will be higher than the last, which will reflect another week of work and growth added to all the previous ones! We take wine! This is called "*yeridah l'tzorech aliya* – a descent for the purpose of elevation*", a higher and greater elevation than before.

So in the cycle of Shabbat and the week we see an elevated beginning, a descent, a loss of that high level of holiness, but only for the purpose of work: a return to the dimension of the beginning, higher, more inspired, more sensitive; closer to that final Shabbat and better prepared.

5 Putting Life into Perspective

Paysach Krohn

At a fund-raising dinner for a school that serves children with learning disabilities, the father of one of the students delivered a memorable speech, one that touched all who attended. After extolling the school and its dedicated staff, he offered a question: "Everything that God does is done with perfection. Yet my son Shai, cannot understand things as other children do. My child cannot remember facts and figures as other children do. Where is God's perfection?"

The audience was stilled by the query and pained by the father's anguish.

The father continued and answered "I believe that when God brings a child like Shai into the world, an opportunity to realise the Divine plan presents itself. And it comes in the way people react to this child."

He then told the following story:

One Sunday afternoon, Shai and his father came to the *yeshiva* as his classmates were playing baseball. The game was already in progress as Shai and his father made their way towards the ballfield. "Do you think they'll let me play?" Shai asked his father.

Shai's father knew his son was not at all athletic, and that most boys would not want him on their team. But Shai's father understood that if his son were allowed to play it would give Shai a much-needed sense of belonging.

Shai's father approached one of the boys in the field and asked if his son could play.

The ball player looked around for guidance from his teammates. Getting none, he took matters into his own hands and said, "We are losing by six runs and the game is already in the eighth inning. I guess he can be on our team and we'll try to put him up to bat in the ninth inning."

In the bottom of the eighth inning, Shai's team scored a few runs but was still behind by three. At the top of the ninth inning Shai put on a glove and played in the outfield.

Although no hits came his way, he was obviously ecstatic just to be on the field, grinning from ear to ear as his father waved to him from the stands. In the bottom of the ninth inning, Shai's team scored again. Now, with two outs and the bases loaded with the potential winning runs on base, Shai was scheduled to be the next at bat. Would the team actually let Shai bat at this juncture and sacrifice their chance to win the game?

Surprisingly, Shai was told to take a bat and try to get a hit. Everyone knew that it was all but impossible, for Shai didn't even know how to hold the bat properly, much less how to connect with the ball. However, as Shai stepped up to the plate, the pitcher moved in a few steps to lob the ball in softly so Shai should at least be able to make contact.

The first pitch came in and Shai swung clumsily and missed. One of Shai's teammates came up to Shai and together they held the bat and faced the pitcher waiting for the next pitch. The pitcher again took a few steps forward to toss the ball softly towards Shai.

As the next pitch came in, Shai swung at the ball and hit a slow ground ball to the pitcher. The pitcher picked up the soft grounder and could easily have thrown the ball to the first baseman. Shai would have been out and that would have ended the game.

Instead, the pitcher took the ball and deliberately threw it on a high arc to right field, far beyond the reach of the first baseman.

Everyone started yelling, "Shai, run to first, run to first!" Never in his life had Shai run to first base. He scampered down the baseline wide-eyed and startled.

By the time he reached first base, the right fielder had the ball.

Everyone yelled, "Run to second, run to second!" The right fielder could have thrown the ball to the second baseman for a tag, but he understood what the pitcher's intentions were, so he threw the ball high and far over the third baseman's head.

Shai ran towards second base as the runners ahead of him deliriously circled the bases towards home. As Shai reached second base, the opposing shortstop ran towards him, turned him towards the direction of third base and shouted, "Shai, run to third!"

As Shai rounded third, the boys from both teams ran behind him screaming, "Shai, run home!"

Shai ran home, stepped on home plate and all 18 boys lifted him on their shoulders and made him the hero for hitting a 'grand slam' and winning the game for his team.

"That day," said the father, who now had tears rolling down his face, "those boys from both teams reached their level of perfection. They showed that it is not only those who are talented that should be recognised, but also those who have less talent. They helped bring a piece of the Divine plan into the world."

Reproduced from Maggid Books with permission of the copyright holders, ArtScroll/Mesorah Publications Limited.

6   Living Life on a High - Naturally

Jonathan Dove

Feel good, now! Make money, now! Enjoy, now! It is hardly surprising that in an age of microwave meals, fax machines and electronic mail, people grow impatient. We live in an age where people have died in order to ensure that a pizza be delivered in ten minutes or less. Cooking times have been reduced to seconds, data transmission is almost instantaneous, so why wait for anything?

Against this background, it seems logical that people who want to improve their enjoyment of life, might do so in a way that is instantaneous. Alcohol, drugs, cannabis, ecstasy, etc. are obvious choices for someone wanting to feel good, now! They provide instant pleasure. However, drug induced experiences tend to be distinct from actual reality. In a personal correspondence with the author, Sir Anthony Hopkins, a recovering alcoholic, writes, "...little work on oneself is possible when the feelings are anaesthetised by a drug. It is only when clean and sober that true feelings can emerge... Getting sober is essential before self-discovery can begin."

Drugs provide a fanciful overlay that affects the perception of reality but does not modify the actual reality. The distorted effect of a chemically created reality has two drawbacks: one is that it cannot be shared with others. The second is more critical, being that it distorts our ability to function effectively in the real world. Hopkins states, "I thought alcohol was the rocket fuel that powered my acting. Actually it was burning me up." False, foolish and superficial... but instantaneous!

In Judaism, man is defined not as *Homo sapiens*, a member of the ape family with more intelligence, but as *Homo Spiritus*", a qualitatively different creature by virtue of having been created with a Divine soul. The most critical area where this spiritual component of man manifests itself is in the area of free choice. Consequently, misusing or abusing free choice is to forgo our essential spirituality and obscure the Divine quality that comes with being created "in the image of God". Not only can drugs lead to misuse or abuse but also to loss of free choice, even if it is only in connection with that particular substance.

Unlike drugs, the focus of Judaism is not simply on feeling good, but on doing good.

So to live life to its fullest is to function properly as a human being, as a Jew and as an individual. Functioning properly and being creative is something that in itself leads to feeling good in every well balanced personality. Our goal as Jews is to elevate the mundane to the sublime, finding sparks of spirituality in every aspect of our lives, our *real* lives. This is done through Torah, *mitzvot* and *middot*.

7 Dinosaurs and the Age of the Universe

Gerald Schroeder

If the Bible is true, then what about Dinosaurs? Scientists claim that those huge beasts lived hundreds of millions of years ago, and were probably destroyed by meteors from outer space some 65 million years ago. But the Bible doesn't even give us 6,000 years for all that to have happened. So which it true, Bible or Science? Admittedly, an Infinite God could have put the world together, dinosaurs and all, in six days, but from a human perspective, 15 billion years seems more logical as the duration of the Universe's existence, especially if we look at all the artifacts Natural Science has discovered. Could the two views somehow both be true?

Rambam, in the introduction to his *Guide For the Perplexed* (1190CE), tells us that if we want to understand how God runs the world – he calls this 'the Science of God' (*madah Eloki), –* we must first understand the 'Science of Nature' (*madah tevah).* And for the Science of Nature, the past century has been a window of revelation. Truths previously undreamed of have changed our comprehension of the nature of time, space and matter.

Let's take Rambam's advice and study a bit of nature. Of course in this pursuit, we'd best first understand the Torah itself – the oldest account of the creation of Nature. The Book of Genesis opens with an account of the first six days, each moving from evening to morning. The passage of time within those days however, is totally abstract. Additionally there is no description of when – within each day – any act of creation took place. Only with Adam and the ensuing progeny of humankind does the Torah relate time to specific events. "Adam lived 130 years and had a son ... Seth. ... Seth lived

105 years and had Enosh" … (Genesis 5:3).

As such, Judaism teaches that Rosh Hashanah (the New Year) relates to the creation of Adam (Genesis 1:27) and not the creation of the universe (Genesis 1:1). The Biblical calendar that reached 5765 this past Rosh Hashanah, is thus based upon dates *from Adam onward;* Time is uniquely linked to Human activity. Since these six days are separate from the other 5765 years, we might plausibly say that the six pre-Adam days were really not days and that the Bible used the term 'day' as a metaphor for long periods of time, epochs, eras.

However according to Rashi[1] and Nahmanides[2] the word 'Day' as used in Genesis chapter one, clearly means 24 hours, and the six days correspond to the six days of our work week. They add however, that these six – 24 hour – days "contain all the days of the world" (Nahmanides Exodus 21:2; Leviticus 25:2). How? And what about the dinosaurs?

To return to the text, each of the six days of Creation close with the phrase "and it was was evening and it was morning …, one day, a second day, a third day, a fourth day…". Nahmanides asks why the Torah wrote *'one day'* in place of the *'first day'*? The latter would be consistent with the numbering of all the other days. Paul Joshua, a student in one of my classes gave the perfect explanation, but in more modern terms. The Bible states 'one day' for the same reason that during the First World War, no one called it WWI – it was called the Great War instead. Simply put, only after the second war, did the Great War become the first.

This logic can be applied to Nahmanides' reading of 'one day'. True, the Torah was given on *Mount Sinai* thousands of years after Creation, and therefore much of the Torah is written in retrospect. However, for the first six days the Torah views time with a *forward-looking* perspective, a perspective from which it could not write of a first day.

The universe at its big bang creation was no larger than the pupil of an eye, packed with all the energy that will ever be, as the Midrash (Leviticus 8:3) and Science both point out. That speck of energy/space expanded, stretching the dimensions of the universe. And in that flow, a fraction of the created energy condensed and became the first stable matter; the protons and neutrons from which the nuclei of all atoms eventually formed. Nahmanides states that "when matter formed, Time grabbed hold." The 6-day clock of the Bible starts (grabs hold) when the first stable matter is formed.

We look back in time and see 15 billion years of history. And those years actually went by. But how would those years *appear* from the perspective of the Bible, from the beginning looking forward? Just as projecting forward in time, the universe would be seen to be getting larger, whereas projecting back in time, the universe becomes smaller and more compressed, so too Time stretches into longer sessions, the further away we are from that point of Creation. And most amazingly, science has discovered that the perception of time is stretched or compressed in exactly the same proportion as the stretching or compression of space during that period. In the jargon of astronomers, these changes are referred to as red shifting and blue shifting (Peebles, Principles of Cosmology, Princeton U. Press, 1993; pp 91, 96).

Astronomy coupled with physics tells us that the universe has stretched a trillion-fold (that's a million million) since the formation of the first matter. Don't take my word for it, consult any standard text on astronomy (J. Silk, The Big Bang; W. H. Freeman, NY, 1989, p 72). What we measure as a trillion seconds of history would appear as one second from the Torah's perspective on Day One. A trillion minutes as one minute; a trillion days as one day. We see a universe some 14 to 16 billion years old. But from the Torah's perspective, those 15 billion years would be compressed a trillion-fold. Fifteen billion years divided by a trillion just happens to equal… 5½days!

It seems the Torah got it right from the start. With the creation of Adam (half way through the 6th Day), the Torah abandons this cosmic view of time and takes up earth-time. From there on in, there are human beings living within Time, and Time has to reflect the people who measure it. Because of this we have always had a two-part Biblical calendar – one with ample time to fit in the dinosaurs.

Notes:

1 Rashi: Hagigah 12a
2 Nahmanides (Ramban): Spain/Israel 1194–1270
   (Genesis 1:3)

8 Israel: a Jewish State or a State for Jews?

Gideon Sylvester

Holidaymakers who visit Israel for the first time enjoy the sunshine, the stunning scenery and the fascinating historical and religious sites. But many of them are perplexed when they discover that most Israeli Jews are not fully observant and much of what goes on in Israel is not in keeping with Jewish tradition. These tourists return home after their wonderful holiday asking, is Israel a Jewish state or simply a state for Jews to live in?

Let us look back in time to the 1890's and to the founding father of the Jewish State: Theodore Herzl. Herzl did not have a religious upbringing, his Zionism emerging only from his experiences working as a journalist at the trial of a French Jew, Alfred Dreyfus who had been falsely accused of treason. When he saw Parisian mobs screaming "Death to the Jews" outside the military barracks at Les Invalides, he understood that despite having full legal rights, Jews were not welcome in nineteenth century Europe. His search for a solution to the problem of anti-semitism began with a plan to convert all the Jews to Catholicism. Without Jews, he reasoned, there would be no more anti-Semitism. Realising eventually, that this would not be practical, he decided that the only way to protect Jews was to find a place in the world where he could establish a Jewish country modelled on the European states.

Herzl's political Zionism was not based on religious ideals, and yet it encapsulated one of the most sacred Jewish values; *Pikuach nefesh;* the principle that to save life is one of the greatest religious acts. "One who saves a single Jewish soul," declared the rabbis "is compared to one who saved the whole world."[1] Herzl's vision has enabled persecuted Jews from the former Soviet Union, from the Displaced Persons camps in post-war Germany, and from the Arab lands to find a haven in Israel. Had it come to fruition in his lifetime, perhaps millions more Jewish lives would have been saved.

However, the idea that it is important for Jews to live in the Land of Israel did not originate with Herzl. The Torah records God's promise to bring the Jewish people to their land, follows their lives there until their enslavement in Egypt and eventual return to the Promised Land. The *Talmud* describes how the ancient rabbis loved the land, celebrated its profound, spiritual qualities and spoke of the enormous privilege of living there. They declared that it was better to live amongst idolaters in the Land of Israel than amongst righteous people elsewhere. Even in the Diaspora, our synagogues are always built facing towards Israel and every major prayer that we say ends with a request for God to return the Jews from the four corners of the earth to their homeland.

Furthermore, Rav Kook, Chief Rabbi of pre-state Israel, believed that the impending birth of a Jewish state marked the culmination of thousands of years of prayer and yearning to return to the Land. He recognised the contribution of the secular pioneers who founded the country, but argued that the country must aspire to reflect Jewish ethics in every area of life. It should reflect righteousness in its laws, compassion in its social policies, creativity in the arts and spirituality in its education policy. This would be a Jewish state in the fullest sense which would enable the Jewish people to flourish.[2]

But even if we fall short of Rav Kook's ideal vision, Israel is still a democracy and most Israelis are traditional, even if not fully observant. Most buildings carry *Mezuzot*, most of the food sold in the country is kosher and Shabbat and festivals are observed as national holidays. By definition, Israeli Jews are immersed in Jewish life and unlike their counterparts in the Diaspora, their chances of assimilating or intermarrying are minimised. For those who wish to live more religious lives, Israel provides unparalleled opportunities to do so, as it has more centres of Jewish learning and living than anywhere else in the world. And whilst there are serious gaps in the Jewishness of the state, there are no quick remedies available, given that imposing religion on a population unready for it would be to court disaster. Genuine Torah must be learned with love and accepted voluntarily.[3] And for those who would wish to see Israel as a more Jewish state in the longterm, *aliyah,* the ballot box and Jewish education offer that opportunity.

It is also correct for us to appreciate those in Israel who give up years of their lives and sometimes life itself, so that we can have a Jewish homeland. We need to support them and our country, which has suffered so cruelly from war and terrorism, both by visiting there and by donating to Israeli charities. Whether a Jewish state or perhaps only a state for Jews, Israel is our country and we should be justifiably proud of it.

Notes:

1 Mishnah Sanhedrin 4:5
2 See for example Rav Kook Igrot HaRaayah Volume 1 page 169
3 See for example Rashi's comments on Deuteronomy 6: 5

9 Yad Vashem

Dr James Weiss

Fifteen years ago, Yad Vashem, the Israeli Holocaust Museum in Jerusalem, opened a new wing. It was financed with several million dollars from a wealthy Jewish family named Spiegel living in Southern California. The wing was dedicated to the one and a half million children under twelve who were slaughtered by the Nazis. The list of innocents includes the donors' son.

Rabbi Berel Wein of Monsey, New York went to see the museum and its new addition. "I had seen Holocaust memorials all over the world and I was expecting to see the standard exhibit full of pictures, personal accounts, gruesome statistics," Rabbi Wein said, "I was not prepared to step into the addition the Spiegel family erected."

"I walked into a single enormous underground room. It was so dark I could not see my hand in front of my face. In the middle of the room a single burning candle provided a small dot of light. Mirrors cunningly placed around the room bounced the light of that candle everywhere, transforming one point of light into hundreds of tiny flames. It was a congregation of tiny souls in search of bodies."

"When I walked into that room," Rabbi Wein recalled, "I was enveloped by darkness. My eyes focused on the small dots of light, which did nothing to illuminate the room. They were suspended in mid-air. Then I heard the recorded voice of a man speaking to the visitors. He said nothing profound yet his words struck deeply into my heart. I stood in the blackest of rooms and stared at the light. I began to imagine that I was surrounded by a million and a half children:

"Chaim Smolovitz," said the disembodied monotone, "Vilna, eight years old. Sarah Kleiner, Vilna, eleven years old. David Ratner, Warsaw, four years old. Rosa Klepper, Berlin, seven years old..." the voice read names without an end. Moishe, Ferencz, Alexander, Shaindy, Zipporah, David, Joel, Zoltan... hundreds of thousands of names, taken from the lists of the Holocaust victims which the Nazis had recorded. These were names of Jews who would have been in their forties and fifties today, with children and grandchildren of their own. Names, names, names until I could bear it no longer."

"I never cried so hard in my life," Rabbi Wein continued. "I fled into the blinding Jerusalem sun. Then it occurred to me that they did not call my name. I'm of that age; my name could have been on that list. I just happened to live in Chicago, not Europe. Had my grandfather moved east instead of west, my name could have been on that roster."

"And if I escaped, there is a reason for it. God saved me because I have a special purpose. Therefore, I have to increase my efforts to do something positive for the Jewish people. I don't know what I should do, build more Jewish schools, talk to more Jews, write articles, but I cannot rest until I contribute to the cause of Jewish redemption. I was spared for a reason."

Reproduced from Vintage Wein by Dr James Weiss with permission from the copyright holders ArtScroll/Mesorah Publications Limited.

10 Prayer: Food for the Soul

Dr Jeffrey Cohen

We open our *siddur*. It is an instinctive act that countless generations of our people have done before us and, we hope, will continue to do long after we have quit life's stage. But what about the high proportion of our people who lack faith, and for whom God's presence is not a tangible reality in their lives? Can authentic prayer really be achieved in the absence of such faith, or does it become reduced to a hollow charade? And in that context, is not a charade an act of blasphemy?

Many people, especially those with a rationalistic bent, are uncomfortable with prayer assuming, erroneously, that one has to be 'on God's wavelength' in order to communicate with Him.

I happen to believe that prayer is actually instinctive within humans and as such, serves to bolster belief in the existence of God. Take the analogy of the inarticulate baby. From the moment of birth, nature endows it with the instinctive ability to exploit the cry as a most potent and stirring vehicle of communication, complaint and supplication. The baby senses the parent's absence as much as its presence; and the need, indeed the demand, for that presence to manifest itself is expressed forcefully and volubly by means of the piercing and plaintive cry. That cry is essentially an act of faith in the existence and proximity of 'the hidden parent' and in that parent's ability to supply all needs. The baby may have had but one single experience of the parent's soothing presence but forever after it has faith in that presence; it craves it and believes passionately that its well-being is inextricably intertwined with it. The child that is taken away from its mother at birth will still cry out for that love and attention. It does not wait until its cognitive functions are sufficiently developed to appreciate the parents' relationship to it, and responsibility for its well-being.

It is the same with God's children. Prayer is the ultimate and most developed form of that instinctive infantine cry. And because prayer is instinctive we do not need to work at faith as a prerequisite. If we have serious misgivings whether God is 'out there,' then giving His presence the benefit of that doubt must certainly be the safest bet. If, on the other hand, we are suffused with the conviction that 'God is close to all who call upon Him,' or even if we merely suspect that He is, 'out there,' then the prayerful cry becomes natural and indispensable.

Once we lose our religious self-consciousness and prayer becomes a meaningful daily exercise, once the words and phrases become a familiar part of our daily vocabulary, and bearers of our innermost emotions – carrying heavenward our needs, fears, pleas, hopes, dreams and gratitude – then the cry gives way to the smile of confidence and ultimately to the joy of faith. Then prayer becomes both spiritually therapeutic and physically invigorating.

So, as with the infant, the fact that God – 'the hidden parent' – is not, or does not seem to be, 'present,' is no reason for refraining from a prayerful cry. Quite the contrary: this is precisely when that cry is most urgent.

We talk about the soul, however difficult a concept it is to grasp and define. We sense that it is a spiritual force within us, there to combat the body's natural preoccupation with physical need and pleasure. It is referred to as *'chelek Elokah mima'al'*, 'a part of God on high,' which is a Heavenly-implanted conscience impelling us to aspire toward morality and integrity; it is at the root of our innate quest for spirituality.

Prayer is the language of that soul. Though whether it is the soul that motivates us to pray, or prayer that activates and arouses the soul, is a moot point. Prayer is certainly calculated to put us in the spiritual mood and mode, and to keep our minds and spirit focused 'elsewhere.'

Many advanced cognitive and aesthetic levels of perception may be reached within the mind and emotions of a musical aficionado when he abandons himself to the inspirational effects of a great composition. The novice, on the other hand, might enjoy the music, but his experience can hardly compare, in quality and intensity, with those of the former. It is the same with the seasoned pray-er who knows the meaning of his prayers, who appreciates the cadences and special style of the Hebrew language of prayer, the majesty and relevance of the *tehillim* that figure so prominently in the siddur, and the spirit of sanctity that envelopes those who truly attempt to engage God through prayer.

But there is so much more to prayer. It is our special gift to God; a gift that parallels the sacrifices offered in the ancient *Beit HaMikdash*. The mere taking off of time within our busy daily work schedules is indicative of our order of priorities, of our wish to consecrate at least some of the time that God allots to us, and to offer it back to Him, invested with our love and gratitude. And the prayer that is offered in synagogue is doubly effective, for it also involves a visit and pilgrimage to God's house. There our prayers link up with those of our coreligionists who pray for us, as we pray for them. There we are truly welded together, constituting a *minyan*, a mini-community. There our communal and national aspirations fuse together with our purely personal prayer, so that we identify with and embrace the entirety of Israel within our thoughts, emotions, petitions and praise.

May our prayers and petitions be answered.

11 Okay There is a God, But What's With All the Laws?

Simon Jacobson

Recent surveys show that as many as 80-90% of Americans say that they believe in God, but nearly half say they do not practice a religion.

Being religious may not seem the logical way to bring a person closer to God. If God transcends all limitation and definition, why would the way to relate to God be to impose further restriction and definition on our already finite and constricted lives?

And yet throughout the ages, whenever man has endeavoured to escape the bounds of the mundane and the everyday, he did so by submitting to a structured, even rigid, code of behaviour.

To answer this paradox let's take music as an example. There are only so many musical notes on the scale, and no one, not even the greatest musician, can create additional notes or subtract any. Anyone who wishes to play or compose music must conform to this absolute, immutable system.

And yet, by submitting to this system, the musician is enabled to create music that can touch the deepest place in a person's heart, a place that cannot be described, much less be defined. By using a framework of notes built from a precise, mathematical formula, the musician creates something that transports the listener to a place high above the confines and fetters of everyday life, high above the strictures of physics and mathematics.

If instead of music we consider religion, we might imagine a discipline whose laws are dictated by the inventor and creator of life, by the one who has intimate knowledge of life's every strength and every vulnerability, of its every potential and its every sensitivity.

But why so *many* laws? Why must this discipline dictate how we are to wake and how we are to sleep, and virtually everything in between?

Because *all* of life, with all of its infinite complexity, is our instrument of connection with God. Every 'note' of every 'scale' must be exploited to achieve the optimum connection.

Music being our metaphor, we cannot but quote the famous anecdote in which Archduke Ferdinand of Austria remarks to Mozart, "Beautiful music, but far too many notes." To which the composer replied, "Yes, your majesty, but not one more than necessary."

Reprinted with permission from the Meaningful Life Centre

12 How a Nazi's Son Became Jewish

Dr James Weiss

On a trip to Israel, Rabbi Berel Wein attended morning services in a synagogue in Jerusalem. He relates that, unlike his own synagogue, which has benches facing the front of the synagogue, this synagogue had tables and benches, allowing him to face those praying around him. A tall, blue-eyed, blond-haired man and three young blond-haired boys walked in and sat down opposite him.

Noteworthy were their aryan features, as well as the seriousness and intensity of their praying. The children were especially well-behaved and followed the service dutifully without once wavering in their concentration. For Rabbi Wein, accustomed to the more freewheeling American child, it was an unusual experience.

At the conclusion of the prayers, a friend of Rabbi Wein's told him that the blond-haired man was a microbiologist at the Hebrew University who had an extraordinary life story.

"Would you like to hear it?" his friend asked, and without waiting for the Rabbi's reply, called to the blond-haired congregant, "Abraham, this is Rabbi Berel Wein. I'm sure he'd like to hear your story."

The two men shook hands and walked home together. The Rabbi listened to him tell the following story:

"I was born and brought up in Germany. My father was an officer in the elite Gestapo killing squad, the Todtenkopf (Deathhead Squad). He served throughout the war and after it was over, successfully eluded capture. But his crimes were so heinous that years later the West German Republic continued to pursue him. He was finally caught and imprisoned for ten years. However, as he was so old, they reduced his sentence letting him out after four and a half years. My father never talked about his past but once he was caught, I read about his crimes for the first time in the newspaper.

Our family was shaken by the news. It was bewildering to find out that my father had led such a monstrous life. I was a teenager and became very confused by all the notoriety. When we went to visit him in prison I couldn't go in to see him. I felt as if he had betrayed me. However, one useful thing came out of this – I developed an interest in the war and found out as much as I could about the Todtenkopf and its role in the Holocaust.

All this occurred around the time the Eichmann trial was taking place, and Holocaust material was beginning to be published. I read all I could find and was able to get a general picture of what happened to the Jews. What I discovered horrified me and the thought that my father played a role – a leading role in the slaughter – made me feel that perhaps our family was tainted with evil. If conditions were the same, I asked myself, could I too become a killer?

I took a trip to get as far away from Germany as possible. It was as if I was haunted by Germany and all things German. I remember that I didn't even want to read Germany history. If Germany could do what it had done in the Holocaust, then its past wasn't usable. It could give us nothing to live by in the future, and studying its history would do more harm than good.

On my journey, I decided to visit Israel to get some perspective on the Nazi's victims and find out what was so special about the Jewish nation that so consumed Hitler. I needed to come to terms with what was churning inside of me. I toured the country, working periodically on agricultural settlements.

While on a *kibbutz*, I saw a poster advertising a summer programme at Hebrew University in desert zoology, and enrolled. I did very well and was able to register for a graduate programme, later earning a PhD in microbiology. While engaged in graduate work, I also became interested in Judaism, and after about two years of studying the religion I decided to become a Jew. Eventually, I married and settled in Jerusalem.

My wife was a German Lutheran, but she too converted. A psychologist might interpret my conversion as sublimating my guilty feelings, but I prefer to think of it as fulfilling my Jewish destiny. Don't ask my how or why, but here we are – an observant Jewish family. And we are happy living as Jews.

About a year ago we learned that my father was not well. My wife thought it would be a *mitzvah* to visit him and finally introduce him to his grandchildren. At first I was apprehensive about going back to Germany, a country I now feared. But, in the end, I took a sabbatical and we went back to Darmstadt to visit my father. It was quite a scene. My boys wore their *kippot*, and had their *tzitzit* showing. Their *payot* were tucked back behind their ears and, of course, they spoke Hebrew.

When my father first saw us, he was overwhelmed, and initially, couldn't bring himself to embrace anyone. However after we talked a bit he seemed to be pleased by the way things were turning out for us.

My father was now over ninety, and I wanted to know why he had merited such a long life with such grandchildren. I asked him point blank what he had done to earn this good fortune. I explained to him that we Jews believe that there are consequences to what we do and the reward system in life is measured very carefully. He looked at me, pondering the question.

He answered, "I can't think of anything outstanding but once in Frankfurt when we were rounding up the Jews, I had the chance to save the life of three Jewish boys who were hiding in a Catholic orphanage. For some reason they aroused my sympathy. I was touched by their plight; they were so lost and forlorn. I felt pity for them, so I allowed them to flee. I don't know what happened to them. But I didn't kill them."

I thought his answer over and told him that according to our tradition his answer made sense. I added, "You know, papa, if you had let four boys go, you would have had four grandchildren."

Reproduced from Vintage Wein by Dr James Weiss with permission from the copyright holders ArtScroll/Mesorah Publications Limited.

13 Why Jews Can't Be For Jesus

Shmuel Arkush

You walk down the road, past people standing on busy street corners who are handing out leaflets. Normally you ignore them, but today, feeling somewhat out of sorts, you stop and have a read. Their literature claims that since Jesus was a Jew and preached to Jews, the answer to all your problems is belief in Jesus, something that they claim will actually make you a better Jew!

Sporting names such as 'Jews for Jesus', 'Hebrew Christians' or 'Messianic Jews', they have budgets totalling millions of pounds and they are energetically targeting Jews. Of special interest to them are those who feel a lack of fulfilment in their lives.

But what is actually wrong with being a Jew for Jesus? In fact, one of the points you hear people put forward, is that these people seem happy enough with it. They assure you that they aren't going to stop doing any of the Jewish things they were doing beforehand, and they may even do a few more! And even if they end up believing in a false messiah, they'll still be Jewish – won't they?

A bit of history. At the time Jesus lived, prior to the destruction of the Second Temple, there were various sects within Judaism. One of these was led by Jesus. His followers claimed he was the long hoped for redeemer of the Jewish people, the *Moshiach*.

Nevertheless, he was rejected by the mainstream Jews of his time, a generation that included some of our greatest Rabbis. The Christian response was a theology which described itself as the 'new Israel' with a 'new covenant with God' and a 'new Testament' to append to the one which had been Divinely delivered, now renamed 'old Testament'.

This was followed by nearly two thousand years of intense, and mostly unsuccessful, efforts to convert Jews, the 'old Israel', to their beliefs. As a result, hundreds of thousands of innocent Jews were locked up in ghettoes, exiled or killed simply for retaining their values. When a Jew accepts Jesus, therefore, he rejects the history of his people.

However the main problem with becoming a Jew for Jesus is the total contradiction involved in fusing together two incompatible religions. So much so, that by adopting the belief in Jesus a person places themselves outside of the Jewish religion and cannot even be counted for a *minyan*.

Let us examine a few examples of this incompatibility. Christians believe in the Trinity, that God consists of the Father, the Son and the Holy Ghost. Our Torah says though, "Hear O Israel, the Lord is our God, the Lord is One."[1] This statement of faith is recited in the *shema*, placed on our doors in the *mezuzah* and on our hearts and minds in the *tefillin*.

Furthermore, the Torah starts the Ten Commandments with, "I am the Lord your God, who brought you out of the land of Egypt...You shall have no other gods before me".[2] Clearly, Judaism does not allow for any other deities even if we still believe in God. Moreover many Christian prayers are addressed not to God but to Jesus.

Christians also say that Jesus was a prophet who came to change the Torah. But the Torah itself warns us about this and says: "If there arises amongst you a prophet or a dreamer and he gives you a sign or a miracle. And the sign or miracle comes to pass and he calls you saying 'Let us go after other gods, whom you have not known and let us worship them.' You shall not listen to that prophet or dreamer. For God is testing you, to see whether you love the Lord your God with all your heart and with all your soul."[3]

Judaism teaches that the Moshiach will bring about, during his lifetime, a building of the Third Temple and peace to the Jewish people and through them to the whole world. Jesus did none of these things to qualify. Indeed many would argue that he has regressed these aspirations. In order to justify this, they formulated the idea of the 'second coming of Jesus' but this is not supported by the Old Testament.

So, okay you have found new friends who are supportive of you and heap love and concern upon you. Your Jewish friends never acted this way. Suddenly you become important and are the centre of praise and attention. But are you a better Jew, a fulfilled Jew, by accepting Jesus? No. By accepting him you commit a fundamental error. You might have found a temporary prop to help you deal with life and its challenges, but the cost is that you have betrayed your people.

Notes:

1 Deuteronomy 6:4
2 Exodus 20:2-3
3 Deuteronomy 13:2

14 Life After Death

Tzvi Freeman

It turns out that lots of people believe in life after death. Two polls conducted by the Gallup Organization report that 79% of Americans believe that after they die their souls will be judged and sent to heaven or to hell, and that 33% believe in ghosts. An internet poll informs us that 38% of those responding believe in reincarnation (though only 26% think that they themselves will be accorded that privilege).

There's a mixed message in these surveys. While they express a certain optimism regarding continuity of our precious selfhood, they also imply that our present state of existence is doomed to obsolescence. We may live on as a basking or roasting soul, a spooky apparition, or the neighbour's cat; but at a certain point, common wisdom has it, life as we know it will come to an end.

Jewish tradition has a more encouraging scenario. While the Jewish concept of the hereafter includes heaven and hell (though a very different heaven and hell than the cloud-borne country clubs and the subterranean fire pits depicted in cartoons), reincarnation and even *dybuks*, its central feature is *techiat hameitim*, the resurrection of the dead. Techiat hameitim states that in the Messianic Age our souls will be restored to our resurrected bodies. In other words, life as our own soul inhabiting our own body – basically the life we know today – will resume.

But the Sages of the *Talmud* go even further than that, stating that there is a level on which life extends beyond death without interruption. "Moses did not die," they categorically state; "Our father Jacob did not die," despite the fact that "the eulogisers eulogised, the embalmers embalmed, and the gravediggers buried."

Chassidic master *Rabbi Shneur Zalman of Liadi* explains that life as we know it can indeed survive death; the question is only what sort of life is it that we know before death.

When do you feel most alive? What is life to you – a good cup of coffee, the smell of baking bread, a stroll in the park on a sun-kissed day? Or is it the experience of seeing a project you've laboured over for months finally come to fruition, or when struggling to explain something to your child seeing the light of comprehension suddenly come on in his eyes?

Life's pleasures are many and varied, but they can be divided into two general categories: the satisfaction of a personal need or desire, or the achievement of a certain impact on the lives of others. The first category offers many gratifying moments; but nothing can equal the fulfillment that comes when you make a difference in others' lives, when the world becomes different – better, smarter, holier – because of something you've done.

The first category ceases with the interruption of physical life. Once you're dead and buried, there are no more strolls in the park. But your impact on the world continues. If you taught something to someone, that person is now teaching it to someone else. If you acted kindly to someone, that person still feels good about it, is a better person for it, and is acting more kindly to others. If you made the world a better place, that improvement is now being built upon to make the world an even better place.

So does 'life as we know it' extend beyond death? That depends on what you know life as. If life, to you, is getting the most you can of its resources for yourself, you have a limited time in which to get as much as you can, and then the fat lady sings and the curtain falls. If life, to you, is making a difference in the lives of others, you're going to live forever.

15 Preserving the Power of Speech

Holly Pavlov

If someone gave you a very powerful gift, you would treasure it and take care of it. You would read the manual, find out how it works and what would cause damage to it. You would store it properly in order to preserve its strength. And you would use it in appropriate ways.

Of course, you would be grateful to the giver of such a gift. You would thank him for it and let him know how much you appreciate it. But the best display of gratitude would be using the gift to its capacity. In fact, every time you used it properly, it would be an active display of your appreciation.

When God created the human being, He formed him from the dust of the earth, and breathed into his nostrils the breath of life. The dust of the earth is the body of the human being, and the breath that God breathed into him is his soul. This combination of body and soul make man a "living being" [1] different from any other creation. In addition to this, man was given two abilities that differentiate him from animals: speech and a highly developed intelligence.

Speech is not only unique to man, but it is what makes man unique. It provides a mechanism for connecting body and soul and translating intelligence and spirituality into physical reality. While some animals possess some form of intelligence, only man has the ability to understand and analyse what is happening in the world around him while maintaining a distinct sense of self. Speech gives each person tools to break down the walls of self and connect with others, to forge and maintain relationships of closeness and meaning.

Spiritually, intelligence gives man the ability to

comprehend what is expected of him in this world, while speech allows him to communicate with his Creator.

Thus, to the three classifications of "Animal," "Vegetable," and "Mineral," the *Talmud* adds another category: "Speaker." Thoughts, emotions, and yearnings are themselves expressions of intelligence. What differentiates man from animals is his ability to express those thoughts, emotions, and yearnings with language.

When God created the world, He did so with speech; "God said, 'Let there be light!' and there was light." [2] Man, who was created in God's image, creates realities in the same way that God does, through the power of speech. Jewish tradition views words as holding power. Once something is said, the words bring about a change in the world. For instance, we often feel better after talking through a situation. Why is that so? In reality, nothing has changed, yet the act of talking changes the speaker, softens him, comforting him. Speaking words has the power to change what he feels.

This is also true in Jewish law. Merely 'saying something' can change the reality. For instance, when a woman blesses her candles on Friday evening, her words sanctify and usher in the *Shabbat*. In effect, she alters her reality. Prior to her blessing, it was not the Shabbat, and now it is. Similarly, when a groom utters a few words after placing a ring on his bride's finger, his words create a marriage. Until he says the words, he is single; once they are spoken, he is a married man.

Speech, then, creates realities. It effects connections between man and God, between one human being and another, between the ephemeral and the physical.

Thus far, we have dealt with the creation of positive realities, but speech retains the power to create negative realities, even to destroy. A child who is called "stupid" will often behave stupidly, even if he is reasonably intelligent. The word affects his perception of himself. And it goes without saying that harsh words spoken to another person create distance, distrust, and hatred.

The power of words ought to be intimidating. Once

something destructive is said, it is nearly impossible to erase its effects. It is exceedingly difficult to not be affected, even ever-so-slightly, once gossip reaches one's ears. Long after a fight is over and sincere apologies exchanged, words spoken in anger linger. No matter how many times we hear, "But I didn't mean it…" we still believe that, in fact, he did. And that belief can eat away at trust and love, to the great sorrow of the person who wishes he had been able to hold his tongue.

Just as speech can be used to create connections, it can be used deliberately to produce disharmony and dislike. This is a great perversity, an abuse of the greatest gift given to us by God, the gift that defines our very humanity, the gift that differentiates us from animals. In fact, engaging in demeaning speech, gossip or meaningless conversation relieves one of his soul, thus leaving only his animal self. Such speech is an animalistic retreat from the Divine within us.

How do we preserve speech so that we remain human? Our Rabbis teach that silence is the fence that protects speech. Many times, in modern society, we speak merely to fill the void, to be noticed. This type of speech is empty. It has no content, no meaning, and cannot effect connections. Not exactly neutral, it actually can create negative realities. For instance, a natural 'default' type of speech is the sharing of seemingly harmless 'news'.

Therefore, we must train ourselves to think before we speak. We ought to speak only words that are properly motivated, that are directed, purposeful, and well thought out. Prior to speaking, one ought to have the right intentions, have evaluated whether it is an appropriate time to speak, and be sure that one is being properly emotionally sensitive.

Words must be sincere. People sense the truth. They know whether a speaker speaks from self-interest or from genuine caring. Words that come from the heart enter the heart.

"God created man from dust of the earth and blew into his nostrils the breath of life and man became a living being."[1] This living being is a reflection of the Divine. As such, mankind is given the capacity to create realities through his speech and action. Also given freewill, he can choose whether to use his gift to imitate God or to align himself with the animal kingdom. Every time he speaks, he chooses either to use the gift wisely and gratefully or to abuse it. Being mindful of our words and choosing them well, shows an appreciation for the gift we've been given.

Notes:
1 Genesis 2:7
2 Genesis 1:3

16 The Jewish Family

Chief Rabbi Dr Jonathan Sacks

The last four British Prime Ministers, James Callaghan, Margaret Thatcher, John Major and Tony Blair have publicly expressed their admiration for the Jewish family. At the same time the Jewish family has fallen apart. Today, one Jew in three marries out. One Jewish marriage in three ends in divorce. Many young Jews are just not getting married, so that for perhaps the first time in history there is a distinct population of Jewish singles.

No faith has invested marriage and parenthood with such significance, spirituality and beauty as has Judaism. The book of Genesis takes just one chapter to describe the creation of the universe. The remaining forty-nine chapters are devoted to variations on the theme of the family, because it is here, in our closest and most sacred relationships, that we create a human universe and try to make it a home for the Divine presence.

What is remarkable about the Torah's treatment of Adam and Eve, Abraham and Sarah and the others is that these are no fairy tale romances. There is hardly a family in the Bible without its conflict and pain. There is nothing infallible about marriage, the Torah seems to say. As proof it sets before us scenes of conflict between husbands and wives, parents and children and between siblings. Yet the Torah is equally insistent that there is no alternative to marriage and parenthood. Adultery and promiscuity are the human equivalents to idolatry.

How then do we make marriage work? Judaism's answer, unrivalled in its power, is to surround it with disciplines and rituals, education and a structured rhythm of expressions of love. The laws of *Shabbat*, the festivals, *kashrut, mikveh*, education and parent-child relationships result in a home life as carefully constructed as a Bach fugue and as breathtaking in its beauty. A good marriage, is not a happy accident but a work of art. It follows strict laws of composition and orchestration, to which each generation and each family adds its own ornamentation.

As long as we lived under this sacred canopy, we preserved the family intact through the most dissolute ages. There were divorces and unhappy families, as there always will be. But they were as few as is possible given the caprice of human character. We are imperfect and even the most sacred institution will reveal our imperfections. But no other framework of relations has remotely rivalled the Jewish home for its capacity to sustain love and fidelity and pass on to children a sense of historical belonging.

The secret lay in Judaism, not in Jews. For no sooner had we abandoned the protective canopy of *halachah* than our marriages became vulnerable and fragile. Today the average Jew divorces as frequently as anyone else. Our community contains cases of child abuse, abandoned families and battered wives. In this individualistic age we have found difficulty in the idea that there are laws governing relationships. The result is that in an age of relative plenty, human happiness has become scarce.

No less seriously, we have discovered that halachah alone will not succeed unless we internalise Judaism's ethic of love. On television recently a psychologist argued that the skills of marriage and parenthood should be made part of the national curriculum. But they were always at the heart of the Jewish curriculum, and we have begun to rediscover them. We need a reminder of the heritage we once had and are now beginning to lose: the Jewish family, our most precious work of art.

17 Kosher - The Ingredients for Life

Jeremy Conway

It is most remarkable that the first command given to Adam is, "From all the trees of the garden you may eat, but from the tree of knowledge of good and evil, you may not eat."

The first command and eventually, the first sin are over food! And when the Children of Israel are given the detailed recipe for life, the Torah, they are handed no less than 28 *mitzvot* about food.

There are laws concerning which types of animals and fish are kosher and about their method of slaughter. There is also the prohibition against consuming blood, the separation of milk and meat, the required waiting time between your steak supper and your cocoa and the prohibition against consuming insects etc.

We can see, therefore, that in Judaism food is an integral part of life. But why are the *kashrut* laws so central to and so critical for Jewish life? Many reasons are given, but I will share with you just two.

The first idea was related to me by an elderly businessman who recalled that for many years he'd brought *kosher* sandwiches to the office for lunch and had once been challenged by a colleague as to the purpose of the finicky kashrut regulations. He responded, "Sam, you're old enough to have been conscripted to the army. Remember what we did every day? Six a.m., on the parade ground, boots polished, buttons spic and span and then tramping back and forth for an hour, right, left, right left, about turn… and all to what end? So that when we found ourselves in the trenches and the sergeant major roared, 'Okay, lads, let's go! Over the top,' our sense of discipline would be so strong, our obedience to his commands so ingrained in our psyche, that we wouldn't even think about it and we'd do what we knew was required of us."

Eating is an activity people indulge in all day, every day, from breakfast to coffee, elevenses, lunch, another snack, and then to another coffee! So that people brought up from childhood keeping kosher have a discipline ingrained within them – checking ingredients, checking their watches to see if they are 'milky', deciding this be can eaten, this cannot. As a result, when they come to face major ethical dilemmas in business, for example, or a severe moral temptation in their social life, they will already have created a disciplined and ingrained sense of identity in their subconscious, "I am a Jew, and these are not my ingredients for life."

There is another more mystical reason for the primacy of kashrut in Jewish life.

"You are what you eat" is a well known saying endorsed by Rabbinic teachings. Summing up the kashrut rules, the Torah states, "These foods you may eat…these you may not…so that you shall sanctify yourselves and be holy."[1] The *Talmud* explains that eating non-kosher food clogs up the arteries of the soul.[2] We are, it seems, spiritually allergic to non-kosher foods, the consumption of which impairs our performance as Jews.

Today everyone is familiar with the reality that you are what you eat; that even a tiny amount of E127 or E124 can affect the behaviour of a hyperactive child, and how carefully the celiac and the lactose intolerant must examine their ingredient list. Which school today has not been designated a nut-free zone? Even the tiniest amount of a problematic ingredient can affect someone's health, their behaviour and even their personality! And so it is, with our inner personality, our spiritual sensitivity; the Talmud teaches that even the tiniest non-kosher ingredient can affect us. Therefore, traditional Jewish wisdom teaches us to eat what is healthy, not just for the body, but also for the soul! Other religions teach about self denial or avoiding hedonism. Judaism teaches the *integration* of body and soul.

In our morning prayer, there is a blessing thanking God for

giving us a healthy, functioning body. "Blessed are you God who heals all flesh and does so wondrously." The meaning of the phrase "and does so wondrously" is that God takes physical flesh and combines it with the pure soul. This is the genius of the wisdom of the Torah, that it understands the intertwined nature of body and soul, and teaches us how to live lives which integrate body and soul, spirituality and worldly reality.

Were it not for this, we'd be no different to the animals. The animals breathe; we breathe. The animals eat; we, too, eat. However, note the different emphasis in the Torah between the creation of man and the creation of animals. When creating animal life God says, "Let the earth bring forth the living creatures... let the waters swarm with living creatures." With the creation of Adam, however, God says, "Let us make man..." Who is "us"? The Rabbis suggest that God is again addressing the earth, and saying, let us jointly create a unique being. "You, Earth, provide the physical flesh, whilst I, from heaven, will infuse it with the spiritual soul."

Thus, the first commandment to man is to remember that he is not an animal but a synthesis of earthly and spiritual elements. The most physical of activities must have a spiritual dimension. Following the kashrut laws, the *ingredients for life,* ensures that not just eating but living, is suffused with a spiritual dimension.

Notes:
1 Leviticus 11
2 Talmud Yoma 39a

18 What Does Belief in God Mean?

Gideon Sylvester

When I first studied in *yeshiva*, I had a crisis of faith. It was *Yom Kippur*, the holiest day of the year and overwhelmed by homesickness and the emotion of the prayers, my mind filled with doubts. I longed to leave the yeshiva and get on the first plane home. A rabbi took me aside and said, "Don't worry, anyone who tells you that they have never had questions is either a fool or a liar!"

The first of the Ten Commandments is to believe in God.[1] For some this comes naturally and presents no problem at all, but for others it is a great struggle. Many Jews have been taught that belief in God is a prerequisite for practicing their religion. They feel excluded from living Jewish lives because, despite their best efforts, they have no idea how to believe in an invisible God. But Judaism acknowledges that faith is not always easy. Thinking people will always have difficult questions.

Having questions is not incompatible with having faith in God, nor does it exclude us from fulfilling His commandments. But who is the God that we must believe in?

Our Rabbis describe how God appears differently in different circumstances. When the Jewish people were freed from Egypt, they perceived God as a Redeemer from slavery. When they saw their enemies defeated, they viewed Him as a warrior, and when they received the Torah on *Mount Sinai* they understood God as Divine ruler. No single perception of God is correct, for, by definition, God is far greater than we can imagine. Each of us captures just a small part of the truth and so each of us will perceive God differently. That's why at the giving of the Torah, even though every Jew was present at the same time in the same place, each one felt that God was talking to him personally and each understood Him in his own unique way.[2]

These ideas liberate us to develop our own personal understanding and relationship with God. *Chassidic* thought stresses the idea that a person should develop their own relationship with God without feeling bound by society.[3] It does not happen all at once. Faith is not something that we are born with or without. It is a journey which can take a lifetime. As we grow older so our understanding of God matures. But how does one embark on the journey?

One way, immediately accessible to us all, is through nature. The *Rambam* describes how the love of God is acquired when a person examines the world and feels overwhelmed by its grandeur and its awesome beauty. These feelings, which we often call spiritual, are classified by the Rambam as the love of God. Many people sense the Divine in history too. In modern times for example, the extraordinary events surrounding the foundation, survival and flourishing of the State of Israel against all the odds points to a Divine hand in history.[4] But whilst these experiences may further belief in God they do not elucidate God's nature. For that we need to turn to Jewish sources.

When we want to find out more about God, we need to turn to His book, the Torah. Its narrative and laws give us an insight into how God sees the world and how we should act in it. However, although Judaism encourages us to devote some time every day to the study of Torah, this alone is not enough. We must also put our thoughts about God into practice by performing the *mitzvot* to the best of our ability. By doing so our actions put us on the path to faith.[5] This is illustrated by a wonderful passage in the *Jerusalem Talmud* which quotes God as saying, "If only My people would forget about Me and keep My commandments."[6] It is through our actions that we reach belief.

We can catch glimpses of God through the actions of people living their lives in a Godly way. When families sit together around Friday night tables, singing and talking together, we sense a touch of the Divine. When we practice selfless acts of charity we feel a glow of God's presence, and the Rabbis declared that the full observance of *Shabbat* was so beautiful that it amounted to a taste of the World to Come. Conversely, when we see bullying, cheating, war and mass murder, the banishment of God is also apparent to us. We know that something is amiss with the world.

The Chassidic Rabbi of Kotzk once asked his students "Where is God?" and supplying the answer to his own question, he said "Wherever you let Him in." What it means for a Jew to believe in God is to try to open our lives to Him and to let Him in. To establish His presence within us and to make him a part of our experience of the world around us.

Notes:

1 Exodus XX:2 Rambam Laws of the Foundations of the Torah 1:1-6

2 See Hizkuni's commentary on Exodus XX: 1 based on Midrash Tanchuma 17

3 See for example commentary of Ba'al Shem Tov on Exodus XV: 2

4 For a traditional understanding of God in history see Rabbi Yehudah HaLevi's The Kuzari

5 See Sefer HaChinuch Positive Commandment 16 and Rav Moshe Chaim Luzzato – Path of the Just Chapter 7

6 Jerusalem Talmud Haggigah 1:7

19 The First Chanukah Light in Bergen-Belsen

Yaffa Eliach

In Bergen-Belsen, on the eve of *Chanukah*, a selection took place. Early in the morning, three German Commandants, meticulously dressed in their festive black uniforms and in visibly high spirits, entered the men's barracks. They ordered the men to stand at the foot of their three-tiered bunk beds.

The selection began. No passports were required, no papers were checked, there was no roll call and no head count. One of the three pointed in the direction of a pale face, while his mouth pronounced the death sentence with one single word: "Come!"

Like a barrage of machine gun fire came the German commands: "Komme, komme, komme, komme, komme." The men selected were marched outside where S.S. men with rubber truncheons and iron prods awaited them. They kicked, beat and tortured the innocent victims. When the tortured body no longer responded, the revolver was used...

The random selection went on inside the barracks and the brutal massacre continued outside of the barracks until sundown. When the Nazi black angels of death departed, they left behind heaps of hundreds of tortured and twisted bodies.

Then Chanukah came to Bergen-Belsen. It was time to kindle the Chanukah lights. A jug of oil was not to be found, no candle was in sight, and a *chanukiah* belonged to the distant past. Instead, a wooden clog, the shoe of one of the inmates, became a chanukiah; strings pulled from a concentration-camp uniform, a wick; and some black shoe polish, pure oil.

Not far from the heaps of the bodies, the living skeletons assembled to participate in the kindling of the Chanukah lights.

The Rabbi of Bluzhov lit the first light and chanted the first two blessings in his pleasant voice, and the festive melody was filled with sorrow and pain. When he was about to recite the third blessing, he stopped, turned his head, and looked around as if he were searching for something.

But immediately, he turned his face back to the quivering small lights and in a strong, reassuring, comforting voice, chanted the third blessing: "Blessed are You, O Lord our God, King of the Universe, Who has kept us alive, and has preserved us, and enabled us to reach this season."

Among the people present at the kindling of the lights was a Mr. Zamietchkowski, one of the leaders of the Warsaw Bund. He was a clever, sincere person with a passion for discussing matters of religion, faith and truth. Even here in camp at Bergen-Belsen, his passion for discussion did not abate. He never missed an opportunity to engage in such a conversation.

As soon as the Rabbi of Bluzhov had finished the ceremony of kindling the lights, Zamietchkowski elbowed his way to the rabbi and said, "Spira, you are a clever and honest person. I can understand your need to light Chanukah candles in these wretched times. I can even understand the historical note of the second blessing, 'Who wrought miracles for our fathers in days of old, as this season.' But the fact that you recited the third blessing is beyond me. How could you thank God and say 'Blessed are You, O Lord our God, King of the Universe, Who has kept us alive, and has preserved us, and enabled us to reach this season"? How could you say it when hundreds of dead Jewish bodies are literally lying within the shadows of the Chanukah lights, when thousands of living Jewish skeletons are walking around in camp, and millions more are being massacred? For this you are thankful to God? For this you praise the Lord? This you call 'keeping us alive'?"

"Zamietchkowski, you are a hundred percent right," answered the rabbi. "When I reached the third blessing, I also hesitated and asked myself, what should I do with this blessing? I turned my head in order to ask the Rabbi of Zaner and other distinguished rabbis who were standing near me, if indeed I might recite the blessing. But just as I was turning my head, I noticed that behind me a throng was standing, a large crowd of living Jews, their faces expressing faith, devotion and concentration as they were listening to the rite of the kindling of the Chanukah lights. I said to myself, if God, blessed be He, has such a nation that at times like these, when during the lighting of Chanukah lights they see in front of them the heaps of bodies of their beloved fathers, brothers and sons, and death is looking from every corner, yet despite all that, they stand in throngs and with devotion listen to the Chanukah blessing 'Who wrought miracles for our fathers in days of old, at this season'; if, indeed I was blessed to see such a people with so much faith and fervour, then I am under a special obligation to recite the third blessing."

Some years after liberation, the Rabbi of Bluzhov, now residing in Brooklyn, New York, received regards from Mr. Zamietchkowski. Zamietchkowski asked the son of the Skabiner Rabbi to tell Israel Spira, the Rabbi of Bluzhov, that the answer he gave him that dark Chanukah night in Bergen-Belsen had stayed with him ever since, and was a constant source of inspiration during hard and troubled times.

Based on a conversation of the Grand Rabbi of Bluzhov, Rabbi Israel Spira, with Aaron Frankel and Baruch Singer, June 22 1975.

20 Miracles

Yitta Halberstam

It is a hot, dry, windless day. The atmosphere is so stagnant, that the very air shimmers with intense heat. No branches sway, no leaf stirs — all is motionless and still. Against this torpid backdrop, a man, in sharp relief to the indolence of the day, is seen rushing down the street. Intent on his own personal mission, he does not notice the leaden sluggishness that surrounds him. He is immersed in his own thoughts, and the conspicuous lack of a breeze, the absence of currents rippling through the blades of grass near him, barely intrude upon his consciousness.

Suddenly, on this very day when nothing else moves, a single leaf plummets to the ground. The man pauses for a fraction of a second, but does not stop to wonder *why* or *how*. After all, this is a commonplace, ordinary event that he has just observed, is it not? Leaves glide and drift and float off trees every day, don't they? Nothing consequential has occurred. Just a haphazard, normal act of nature that occurs all the time. The man shrugs his shoulder in indifference and marches on. He does not know that what he has just witnessed is a miracle.

For on the sidewalk beneath the man's feet, a little worm, unseen by the naked human eye, has just cried out to God: "God, it is *so* hot today! I am boiling under the blazing sun! Can't you please send me a little shade?" And God, who has infinite mercy on all his creatures, even tiny worms, responds immediately to the heartfelt plea. But the man, whose vision is limited, whose comprehension is circumscribed, is oblivious to the small drama that has just taken place. He only sees the plummeting leaf; he does not see the worm on the ground. The man is completely unaware of the fact that he has just watched an act of God.

"We do not see things as *they* are," the Talmud tells us, "we see things as *we* are." We human beings filter reality through the prism of our already entrenched beliefs, prejudices, and biases. Our perceptual abilities are enormously affected and influenced by our subjective feelings. Even when we think we are seeing reality clearly, we may not be seeing it at all.

A famous scientist once reported a fascinating phenomenon: He had travelled to the (then) remote island of Micronesia, whose primitive natives had no conception of the realities of the modern world to which we are so inured. The natives were terrified by the electronic products the scientist showed them, convinced that it was some magical power that made them work. But what truly startled the scientist and his team of researchers was the insight they gleaned about the power notpreconceived notions and man's inability to see that which he can't understand. When a platoon of ships sailed near the island of Micronesia and came into view, the scientists excitedly pointed them out to the natives. And then a puzzling, bizarre, unfathomable thing occurred. Although the ships were clearly visible to the scientists, the natives – who had never seen a ship before – could not see them at all. *They did not see the ships because they could not comprehend them.* They were outside the milieu of their experience and thus beyond their perception.

The two stories above, must by necessity, make us feel humble and small, shaking our certainties and confidence. How many of life's mysteries are we really seeing – and grasping? What about its miracles? When we say "Well, nothing miraculous ever happens to *me*," are we perhaps making this statement from a place of unawareness – or ingratitude? Could it be that life is actually permeated with small miracles every day, and we just don't see them? We are finite beings after all; how can we presume to penetrate the infinite mind?

"That which the caterpillar calls the end of life, the master calls a butterfly," the novelist Richard Bach has said. Could it be that the ordinary events of day-to-day life are in fact not plain happenstance, but small miracles instead? How differently we would experience life, if we would live with eyes filled with wonder, considering each day through the prism of "radical amazement" as one theologian described it.

The history of the Jewish people is drenched in miracles: apocalyptic, sublime, grandiose, and breathtaking. Sadly, in contemporary times, we are not privileged to witness the scope and grandeur of God's miracles in the same manner as our forefathers did, but we do experience the "coincidences" that attest to God's presence. These gentle taps on our shoulder remind us that God is with us always, even in the ordinary details of day-to-day life.

We can choose to experience the awe, the mystery, the wonder of a Higher Power orchestrating our lives with infinite care and attention. Through the medium that some mistakenly call "coincidences," we are a party to nothing less than miracles.

May we all be blessed with the wakefulness and wisdom to know them when they come into our lives. We are fuller and better people when we recognise and acknowledge God's hand; we vibrate with joy and gratitude; for God, for the universe, and for all its creatures with whom we are interconnected in a great field of spiritual energy laden with meaning, order, and love.

21 Why Do We Need The Oral Law?

Dayan Yonatan Abraham

To address this issue four questions need to be answered:
What is the Oral Law?
Why isn't the Written Law alone sufficient?
Why wasn't the Oral Law included in the Written Law?
How is it that we do have a written form of the Oral Law today?

What is the Oral Law?
The Oral Law is the collective name for the laws, elucidations, explanations and additional detail taught by God to Moses at *Mount Sinai*, then handed down orally by Moses to Joshua and so on, to and through the outstanding leaders of each successive generation.

They form a comprehensive compendium of information and detail which is the key to correctly understanding the Written Law. By incorporating the scholarship and teachings of generations of Jewish sages, the *Mishnah* and *Talmud* (as the compilations are known) comprise the veritable living soul of the body mass of Torah.

Why isn't the Written Law alone sufficient?
The Oral Law is not limited to merely providing deeper insights of the Torah. Many parts of the Torah are wholly inexplicable without the Oral Law.

Take the Jewish calendar for example. The yearly cycle is crammed with Festivals, High Holydays, days of celebration, commemoration as well as fast days and periods of mourning. All these are predicated on the existence of a Jewish calendar system since they are identified in the Torah as occuring on a specific day of a particular numbered month. However, no detailed instruction appears in the Torah as to how to formulate a calendar, to define a month or calculate a year. How could something of such fundamental importance to so many areas of *mitzvah* observance have been simply 'overlooked' or omitted?

This, writes *Ibn Ezra* in the introduction to his classic commentary on the Torah, presupposes the existence of an Oral Law which indeed gives specific guidance on the formulation of the calendar according to Torah law. In turn this proves the veracity of the Oral Law.

As an additional illustration, take the mitzvah of *Shabbat* observance which, the Torah states, is the sign of the Covenant between God and Israel and therefore plays such a major part in Jewish life, being the spiritual focus which infuses the other six days of the week with both meaning and spirit. Breaching any of its numerous restrictions constitutes a desecration of the special bond between God and Israel and can have severe consequences.

Yet a list of those thirty-nine restrictions, although intimated, does not appear in the Torah! Nor for that matter are the details of *tefillin*, *tzitzit*, *mezuzah*, the marriage ceremony, *bar* and *bat mitzvah*, *lulav* and *etrog*, or the blowing of the *shofar* on *Rosh Hashanah* to name just a few of the numerous areas of basic Torah observance, mentioned in the Written Law.

All the required information and necessary details for all the laws of the Torah appear in the Oral Law. It is thus the indispensable guide to a correct understanding of the Torah. As *Rambam* states in the eighth of his *Thirteen Principles of Faith*, integral to the Jewish Faith is the belief that all of Torah, the Written and Oral Law, is of Divine origin.

Why wasn't the Oral Law included in the Written Law? One reason for this is purely pragmatic; with such a plethora of details, such a variety of applications and so intricate a set of guidelines, inclusion of the Oral Law in the actual text of the Torah would have lead to the principles being lost in the minutiae of detail.

God rather gave us a concise guidebook for life – the Torah – which is similar to a table of contents, alluding to further elaboration, interpretation and application which is to be found in the Oral Law.

On a deeper level though there is a far more significant reason. Whilst the Written Torah became 'public property' when the Bible was adopted by the world at large, the central part of Torah including the depths of its message, the authenticity of its transmission and the accuracy of its application was entrusted to us alone. As the nation which stood proudly and united at Mount Sinai and declared in unison "Na'ase – we will fulfil and scrupulously observe", "Venishma – we will listen to learn and absorb the Oral Law", we alone became the guardians of its transmission. It is uniquely ours. The holy task of perpetuating it through the millennia became the privileged responsibility of the leading sages of each generation.

How is it that we do have a written form of the Oral Law today?

The Oral Law was meant to remain, in principle, unwritten. It was to be transcribed on the hearts of our people and retain expression through the lives of each successive link in the unbroken chain back to its origins at Mount Sinai.

However, in the aftermath of the destruction of the Second Temple (in 70 C.E.) with the shattering effect of the Exile and Dispersion on the citadels of Torah learning in Israel and the waning of Jewish scholarship in general, the ongoing transmission of the Oral Law was itself at risk.

The outstanding rabbinic leader of that era, *Rabbi Yehuda HaNasi*, deemed it necessary to record the whole of the Oral Law in order to guarantee its survival. Accordingly, he convened a gathering of the leading sages of his generation, collated their rulings and decisions and compiled them into the structure that came to be known as Mishnah. This encapsulates the full gamut of *Halacha LeMoshe MiSinai* – the laws Moses brought down from Sinai, which are further expounded and elaborated upon by the following generations of Sages and which is recorded in the Talmud.

The *Shulchan Aruch*, is the codification of the distilled *halachic* essence of the Talmud and is the practical handbook of Torah law as it applies across the spectrum of life's situations.

Today, as we commemorate the holy victims of the Holocaust, we must simultaneously stand in awe at the triumph of the survival of our Torah heritage through the indomitable spirit and amazing dedication of the survivors. We can marvel at and take comfort from the amazing rebirth of Torah scholarship and the re-emergence of centres of Torah learning all around the world, most notably in Israel. Our Jewish schools, *yeshivot*, seminaries and community learning centres are the true repositories of the lifeblood and spirit of the eternal message which makes us a truly eternal people – the eternal Oral Law.

22 Why Did God Create the World?

Moshe Krupka

It's a fair question. Just why would an infinite, all powerful God, unbounded by time and space want to create a universe? In his *Book of Beliefs and Philosophies* the 10th century scholar *Rav Saadia Gaon* gives three suggestions to explain God's creation of the world and its inhabitants.

His first somewhat surprising suggestion is that from a human perspective God had no reason to create the world. This is not to say that creation was a wanton act but rather that God's motivation is beyond human understanding. Although not intellectually satisfying, this suggestion is in good company. All explanations of creation, whether philosophical or scientific, require a leap of faith. That goes as much for Aristotle (wondering where a God-free eternal universe might have come from) as it does for an astrophysicist (scratching their head about the origins of Big Bang Theory's primeval atom). Rest assured, argues Rav Saadia, God had his reasons even if they are beyond us.

Rav Saadia Gaon's second suggestion is that God's creation of the world was a result of properly expressing loving-kindness. The ultimate expression of loving-kindness involves bestowing it on others. From God's point of view, "others" requires a created universe. Thus he created the world so that beings could benefit from their use of the world's bounty. This is alluded to in Isaiah, "...I am the Lord your God, Who instructs you for your benefit, Who guides you in the way you should follow."[1]

The third suggestion comes from Psalm 145 "To inform human beings of His mighty deeds, and the glorious splendour of His kingdom."[2] Here the manifestation of God's greatness and wisdom, rather than his loving-kindness, provides the motivation behind creation.

If we combine these three ideas we begin to see that from our perspective, the act of creation was one through which God expressed Himself. The universe that we are a part of is a canvas for this self expression. This is what is meant by saying that creation serves "to glorify God".

Consider the following *Mishnah* from *Ethics of our fathers*:[3] "*All that the Holy One, Blessed is He, created in the world He created solely for His glory, as it is said: 'All that is called by My Name, indeed, it is for My glory that I have created it, formed it, and made it [4].' And it says: 'Hashem shall reign for eternity.' "*

God hasn't created us because he needs the praise – far from it – we're here because we're part of what makes God God! This amazing realisation gives a clue as to our role in creation.

Rabbi Aryeh Kaplan in *If You Were God* writes the following:

"*To the best of our understanding, God created the universe as an act of love. It was an act of love so immense that the human mind cannot even begin to fathom it. God created the world basically as a vehicle upon which He could bestow His good. But God's love is so great that any good that He bestows must be the greatest good possible. Anything less would simply not be enough.*

But what is the greatest good? What is the ultimate good that God can bestow on His creation?

If you think for a moment the answer should be obvious. The ultimate good is God Himself. The greatest good that He can bestow is Himself. There is no greater good than achieving a degree of unity with the Creator Himself. It is for this reason that God gave man the ability to resemble Himself."

But what is this 'ability to resemble Him' that God gave us? Rabbi Kaplan explains that we can "resemble God" by correctly exercising our free will. We have the power to choose to live the life that God has advocated, the life that allows us to achieve the greatest benefit from His world, a life guided by His Torah and His *Mitzvot*.

And when we do that we become close to God. Indeed we become His partners in creation.

Notes:
1 Isaiah 48:17
2 Psalm 145 verse 12
3 Ethics of our Fathers 6:11
4 Isaiah 43:7

23 How Can We Believe in God After Auschwitz?

Y.Y. Rubinstein

I think that there would be very little debate if I suggested that this question is in fact the question. The pain generated by the Nazis' attempts to end the existence of the Jewish people is almost as real to today's new generation, as it was to the old. I was surprised when I first started dealing with the problems of Jewish students, to find the children and grandchildren of victims still having their lives disturbed, and in some cases destroyed by the Holocaust. The Jewish people have not stopped bleeding.

The question, whether the Holocaust killed belief or not, should have been thought about by every Jew alive. There are some, however, who simply refuse to think.

There is a book which I wish every Jew would read; it is called 'Reunion' and it is by Fred Uhlman. The book is a semi-autobiographical account of the author's adolescence in pre-war Germany. It gives us a rare glimpse into the lives of a not untypical, German Jewish family. In the book, the Jewish boy through whom the tale is told, reports an accident when his neighbour's wooden house went up in flames, burning to death the three children who were inside. He writes:

"It shook me as nothing had shaken me before. I had read of one million people drowned by the Yellow River, of two million drowned by the Yangtse. I heard that a million soldiers died at Verdun. But these children I knew, I had seen them with my own eyes – this was altogether different. What had they done, what had the poor mother and father done to deserve this?

"It seemed to me that there were just two alternatives – either no God existed or there did exist a deity who was monstrous if powerful, and futile if powerless. Once and for all,

I jettisoned all believe in a benevolent mastermind."

In the story, the Jewish boy discusses the issue with his non-Jewish friend who takes it to his Pastor. The Jew is very unimpressed with the answer he receives and there the issue is left. Imagine; someone who boldly declares that he never superseded the intellectual achievements of his adolescent mind. At least the non-Jew takes a theological question to a theologian. Not so the Jew. There are some who refuse to think.

A number of years ago a very angry student asked me how I would answer someone who was religious and who went through *Auschwitz* and declared that there was no God.

The answer of course is, that I would have no answer for him! There is a Jewish teaching which declares that you shouldn't judge someone till you are standing in their shoes. I would however, have a question of my own. "What would that survivor say to someone who didn't believe in God and went through Auschwitz and declared that there is a God?" One of my teachers told me of a non-Jew who actually converted in *Dachau*. A *mikveh* was dug underneath one of the huts, it was filled with rain water and this man was circumcised and became a Jew… in Hell. All of these cases demonstrate one thing unequivocally. The Holocaust proves nothing with regards to the existence of God; it neither destroys belief nor endorses it. I have met a Jew who was created an atheist by Auschwitz. I have met two Jews who had the reverse experience. I have known scores who were and remained Torah Jews, despite the camps.

At almost the end of the Torah[1] God warns *Moses* what will happen after his death: God says to Moses, "When you go to lie with your Fathers and this people will rise up and lust after the alien gods of the Land into which they are coming. And they will abandon Me and break My covenant which I made with them … And My anger will burn against them on that day and I will abandon them and I shall surely hide My face from them and they will be their enemies' prey."

It would seem to be, that the conditions of the contract between God and the Jewish people are spelled out here. If you give me up and chase after other belief systems and "Isms", then My ultimate punishment will be... "O.K you want it, you've got it!" If we choose Nationalism or Socialism and the Nationalists or Socialist turn on us – then the question is no longer "how could God let this happen?"; rather, how could we have let this happen?

In every generation there is an alternative system of belief, available and tantalising to Jews. The "Ism" comes along, offers itself and carries off thousands and sometimes millions of adherents. The contract we have with God is simply the availability to embrace the new "Ism" ... but it has to be a full embrace, with all that it implies, if this alternative fails us, then we have to bear the consequences; we chose it.

There is a phenomenon which I call "The solitary remaining Jewish advocate." After an "Ism" has proven itself bankrupt and failed, you will find solitary remaining Jewish advocates, arguing that their particular fossil is still vibrant, alive and necessary.

The place where I studied in *yeshivah* is a very anti-Semitic part of the world. I was once visiting Manchester and went into a Jewish bookshop belonging to a Mr Falk. The owner was someone whom I admired greatly. He was a German Jew and his children are amongst some of the most outstanding in the Rabbinic world. The shop was empty and he asked me how I was getting on in yeshivah. There had just been a particularly ugly anti-Semitic incident and I decided to tell him the whole story. Once I started it all came gushing forth. This was in the late seventies and the National Front were doing really well. I was sickened and fed up within being spat at, shouted at and occasionally attacked. Mr Falk invited me to sit down and began to tell his own story.

"My wife and I were in Buchenwald. It was a place which took people and ground them into tiny bits. When they rounded us up we were marched to the railway station where thugs with wooden staves waited to meet us. The cattle trucks which were to take us to the camps stood with their doors open. We were told that we had to shout (here he mentioned a long German word which apparently combines all the worst swear words into one). If we shouted that we were that word, then we were allowed to pass unmolested by the thugs." Mr Falk shouted it and when he was squeezed into the cattle truck he found himself beside someone who had blood pouring from a gash in his forehead. The man who had refused to give in asked Mr Falk how he could have brought himself to say it. It took me a number of years to understand what Mr Falk replied; it was this… "I said it because it didn't touch me".

The train moved off, travelling through the birthplaces of some of the great philosophers and composers that all the Jews on the train had been brought up to be so proud of. When they arrived at Buchenwald, Mr Falk said that he thought, "I don't know why God has put me here but it's my job to get on with being a Jew here, just as much as it would be anywhere else"; and then he said something which astonished and inspired me: "And with that attitude, I was able to help very many people". Imagine – Buchenwald, where human beings were reduced to animals; being able to help very many people.

The answer to the riddle of his reply to the casualty in the cattle truck, lies in the phenomenon of the solitary remaining Jewish advocate. During the 1930s in Berlin, large numbers of Jews would be found every day who committed suicide. The reason for their suicide can be found in the 'Reunion'.

"I still remember a violent discussion between my father and a Zionist who had come to collect money for Israel. My father abhorred Zionism. It could only end in endless bloodshed and the Jews would have to fight the whole Arab world. And anyway, what had he, a Stuttgarter, to do with Jerusalem?

"When the Zionist mentioned Hitler, and asked my father if this would not shake his confidence, my father said 'Not in the least. I know my Germany. This is temporary illness, something like measles, which will pass as soon as the economic situation improves. Do you really think the compatriots of Goethe and Schiller, Kant and Beethoven will fall for this rubbish? How dare you insult the memory of the twelve thousand Jews who died for our country – fur unsere Heimat?'"

Unable to take being rejected by Germany, Unsere Heimat, Jews gave up their lives. Germany for those Jews was life. That was what the man meant when he asked "How could you bring yourself to say that about yourself?" He couldn't, he was a real German, a patriot; the solitary remaining Jewish advocate. Mr Falk could say it because it didn't offend him, his life wasn't being a German, it was being a Jew.

A memo was sent by Gestapo headquarters in Berlin to Gestapo H.Q. in Poland. It said that the Nazis were willing to allow some Jewish emigration from Germany and Austria, because the assimilated Jews of Western Europe would simply blend into whatever country was willing to accept them; there was no danger that they would re-establish Jewish life in their new surroundings. From Eastern Europe, however, no escape was to be permitted. The Ostjuden were too Jewish, they would rebuild their institutions and start all over again. This they could not permit.

Hitler put it this way: "It is true that we are barbarians. That is an honoured title to us. I free humanity from the shackles of the soul, from the degrading suffering caused by the false vision called conscience and ethics. The Jews have inflicted two wounds on mankind – circumcision on its body and conscience on its soul. They are Jewish inventions. The war for the domination of the world is waged only between the two of us, between these two camps alone – the Germans and the Jews. Everything else is but deception."

I am proud to be, by their own definition of their antithesis, the opposite of a Nazi, a "too Jewish Jew". Every "Ism" has eventually failed us. When we have insisted that God withdraws, then we have been shown by that in which we put all our trust, how wrong we were. The question "How can we believe in God after Auschwitz?" begs another reply, "After Auschwitz, how can we believe anything else?"

Notes:
1 Deuteronomy 31:16-18

24 The Secret of Jewish Survival

Aubrey Hersh

No other nation has experienced a past quite like ours. In the 4,000 years from Abraham to the present day (three quarters of the entire history of civilised humanity!), we have wandered the world, seeking our fortunes. And with only a few happy hours intervening amidst long periods of suffering – powerless, despised and persecuted – the Jewish people have nevertheless enriched the nations of the world morally, religiously and economically. Even Christianity itself is inconceivable without Judaism.

But how? How did we rise from the expulsions, the pogroms, the exiles and, more recently, from the Holocaust?

We must conclude that it is not due to any peculiar characteristic, location or language, since none of these have been a constant. The Jews in Yemen, Germany and Spain shared neither dress nor geography and certainly not language.

Our answer really starts with the past, which sadly, we know perilously little of. Ironically, we learn of the Crusades in school and cheer the victories of Richard the Lionheart, though as Jews, our hopes and survival actually lay with Saladin. [1] We are unaware of our own history: how Jews upheld their dignity both as human beings and as Jews, of the great lives that were lived by ordinary Jewish people. Our ignorance about our own history obscures the miracle of our survival. More's the pity, for in that survival lies a message for us today: the message of memory.

Only through memory do we have a clue as to who we are and what we are here for. We need to live with an eye on the past.

Yet at the same time, keeping the memories alive, does not

suffice. Our generation has read, seen and heard about the Holocaust, and our exposure to it is comprehensive, yet in this generation we are experiencing the highest assimilation and dropout rate in our collective history. Because the secret of survival is to maintain memory *in a Jewish way*, which requires looking not just with one eye but with two, not only backward but forward – we need both *memory and vision*.

The proven formula to maintain both memory and vision was shown 2,000 years ago. In 70 CE, with the Second Temple about to be destroyed, the Jews faced the loss of their autonomy and independence, and it was left to the sage *Rabbi Yochanan* to resurrect the Jewish people. The *Talmud* records how, having smuggled himself out of Jerusalem and obtained an audience with the Emperor Vespasian, he made one crucial request: "Spare our houses of learning," they are our link both to our past and to our future, they are our *Memory* and they are our *Vision*.

Alan Dershowitz – a renowned American lawyer and author, sums it up thus:

"We are the people of the book. Our collective library is unparalleled. In every nation in which we have lived, we have taught, written, created, invented, and left an intellectual legacy. Ahad Ha'am, one of the greatest non-religious Jewish thinkers in modern history, declared in 1910 that 'the secret of Jewish survival is learning, learning, learning.'"

Dershowitz adds that in light of this long commitment to learning, it is sadly remarkable that:

" ...no group in America is less knowledgeable about its traditions, less familiar with its language than the Jews. We are the most ignorant and illiterate of Americans when it comes to knowledge of the Bible, the history of our people and religious traditions. More Jews can tell you the name of Jesus' mother than Abraham's father. More Christians than Jews can recite the Ten Commandments. We get our history from Fiddler on the Roof, our traditions from canned gefilte fish, our Bible stories from television, our culture from Jackie Mason, and our Jewish morality from the once-a-year synagogue sermon most of us sleep through." [2]

Study allows us as Jews to look at the past and see ourselves, not as victims but as survivors. The danger otherwise as one historian put it, is that our children will learn about the Greeks and how they lived, the Romans and how they lived, and the Jews and how they died.

The current British Chief Rabbi has said: "*The fate of the Jews was, is and predictably will be, determined by their approach to education… Over time, other alternatives were tried and failed, this proposition however, has been tested at critical moments in Jewish history… The Jewish people has never allowed its academies to fail and that is the secret of its immortality.*"[3]

Admittedly this is not a quick fix solution, but neither is the survival of the Jewish people. The historian Rabbi Wein told me of the time he was giving a talk in the States and was to be picked up from the airport. After his driver spent a frustrating 40 minutes searching for the car, they looked at the parking ticket again, only to find they had been searching in the short-stay park, for a vehicle parked in the long-term bay! Rabbi Wein subsequently commented that their predicament actually mirrored that of the Jewish nation. Too many of us are trying to find fulfillment in the short-term section, forgetting that as Jews we are firmly positioned in the long-term parking lot, a fact which the ruins of the Acropolis, Babylonia and Ancient Rome are a mute testimony to. Jewish survival isn't easy, or predictable but neither is it short term.

In 1944 the Nazis marched into Elie Wiesel's hometown. He was baking *matzot* for Passover with his *Rebbe*. The Rebbe sighed, lowered his head for a moment, then turned to him and said: "*The Germans are here you say? Well, let me ask you this. Have you forgotten the meaning of Passover? Our enemies are swallowed up; the People of Israel survive.*" And with that, they continued baking matzot. [4] The nation's survival may not have seemed even remotely possible in March 1944, but 60 years on we live, renewed, and with a vision for our future. As the Russian author Leo Tolstoy wrote in 1908: "*The Jew is as everlasting as Eternity itself… He was the first to produce the Oracles of God and he has been for so long its Guardian, transmitting it to the rest of the world. Such a nation cannot be destroyed.*"

Notes:

1 Saladin (1137-1193) Sultan of Egypt. Saladin was protective of the Jews in his realm and Rambam served as his personal physician.

2 *The Vanishing American Jew* (1997)

3 Studies in Renewal – Rabbi Dr Jonathan Sacks (1993)

4 Tout les fleuves vont a la mer – Elie Wiesel Memoirs Vol. 1 (1994)

25 Jewish Business Ethics

Zvi Leiberman

"The love of money is the root of all Evil."[1]
Rabbi Yishmael said, "One who wishes to become wise should study the laws of money, for there is no area of Torah that is greater; it is like an ever flowing stream."[2]

In our tradition, an object is neither the source of all happiness nor the root of all evil. Rather, it is an opportunity.

The *Jerusalem Talmud* tells us that Moses wondered, "What is the 'holy *shekel*' that was to be used in the building of the *mishkan*?" He was shown a "shekel of fire" taken from beneath God's holy throne.[3] Rabbi Elimelech of Lizensk explains that fire can destroy and annihilate or it can warm those who are cold and bring light where there is darkness. Similarly, money can become an overwhelming burning passion in one's soul that destroys lives and corrupts society, or it can be used to help those in need. It can be used to gratify our basest and darkest desires or it can, bring light, joy and hope to places that would otherwise be dark and miserable. The 'holy shekel' is money correctly used.

The ability to approach money in this way comes through appreciating that it is a plentiful resource that flows from the blessing of God. The Torah introduces the sections devoted to appropriate use of money with an attitude of abundance, "When you reap your land's harvest…"[4] It is only when we believe that something is scarce that we need to hoard it or fight for it. Only when we appreciate that all wealth and sustenance flow from the kindness of God, Whose means are unlimited, can we then transform all that He provides into a 'holy shekel' because we indeed sense that it comes from beneath His holy throne.

This responsibility to make money into a 'holy shekel' sheds a unique insight into our tradition. An entire section of the *Shulchan Aruch* deals with the laws of money including the laws of partnerships, tort, copyright, verbal agreements, fixed tenancy, inheritance, redundancy and trespass. All of these laws seek to elevate money to a 'holy shekel.' The Shulchan Aruch discusses not only how to disperse money as *tzedakah* but also how to accumulate wealth without trampling on others or taking from them what is theirs by right and moral imperative.

The business world is competitive. Our *halachic* tradition defines what is fair and what is unfair competition. We record the rabbinic discussions about when it is legitimate to compete with an existing enterprise and how we prevent ruinous competitive practices that destroy communities and the livelihood of those within them. These laws protect the rights of employees from unscrupulous employers and define the responsibilities of employees to their employers so as not to take unfair advantage of them. They protect consumers from fraudulent pricing and inaccurate weights and measures. It defines the responsibility a business has to the environment and also its the responsibility to protect the lives and welfare of the community from exploitation.

While we may not be able to impose our attitudes on the world around us, by following the values outlined in the Torah and detailed in halachah we can be exemplars of Torah values worthy of emulation, that all can aspire towards. This then makes all our income a 'holy shekel' that is used not only to build the mishkan but to build an entire world in which God's presence can be found.

Notes:

1. I Timothy 6:10 (Christian Bible)
2. Talmud Bava Batra 175b
3. Midrash Tanchuma 9
4. Leviticus 19:9

26 The Long Journey Home

Andrew Shaw

Rosa was born on July 31st 1896 in a small Jewish *shtetl* in Galicia, in what is now present day Austria. When she was just two years old, her father, a rabbi, died, and her mother was left looking after three young girls. Unfortunately while Rosa was still in her teens, her mother also died and the three sisters were left to fend for themselves.

Eventually, they moved to Vienna where they somehow managed to exist.

When Rosa was in her late twenties she met Kalman and after a couple of years, they became engaged. However, due to circumstances beyond their control – Kalman had to support a mother and two sisters back home – they could not get married. Finally, in 1938 when Rosa was already 41 they decided that they should marry despite the circumstances.

In a world about to go mad, two Jewish people made the ultimate commitment to each other, not knowing that their dreams of a happy marriage would be short lived.

With Hitler making advances into Austria it was clear to many people in the Jewish community that staying on would be suicidal and many looked for a way out. As fate would have it, Rosa was given a ticket and a work permit by an old lady who had no need of it – one ticket, away from the nightmare of the Nazi machine closing in. Rosa took the flight to freedom, from where she thought she would be able to help the rest of her family – a family that she never saw again.

The ticket was to a country where she would find no family, no friends, and a language that she neither knew nor understood. She arrived in the winter of 1938 in Glasgow, became ill and was taken to hospital where she found out she was pregnant.

Up until the time her baby was born she was still able to correspond with Kalman. She received a letter from him telling her not to worry, how he was soon taking the last train out of Vienna bound for the safety of Warsaw, and how overjoyed he was about the baby. That was in July 1939! She never heard from him again.

On July 9th 1939 Rosa gave birth to a baby girl whom she named after her late mother, and began the difficult task of raising a Jewish girl in a Jewish way all by herself – not an easy task. And yet, without books, radio, or family, the little girl grew up knowing all about her heritage.

The Holocaust took a tremendous toll on Rosa's family, all of Rosa's family perished in the Holocaust, but neither her spirit nor her indomitable will diminished.

The two of them lived in poverty during the war years, Rosa doing whatever jobs she could find to do, as long as she was free during the day to devote herself to her daughter and to instill in her all those values that she held so dear. Both she and her daughter were filled with awe and exultation the day they heard of the declaration of the state of Israel. For them it was a modern day miracle but both doubted they would ever be able to visit the 'Promised Land'.

In 1949, due to the inclement Scottish weather and the prospect of better educational chances for her daughter, they moved to London.

Mother and daughter had many difficult but happy years together, and then in March 1967, her daughter married. Rosa moved in with the young couple and continued to be a tower of strength.

In December 1968 her daughter gave birth to her first child, a baby boy. Rosa now had a grandson, and three years later, she had two. Her grandchildren, who were brought up in a loving, Jewish environment, were her constant joy, and she spent many hours reading stories to them as they drifted off to sleep. She had endured so much pain during her life, that it was only fitting that in her later years, her days were filled with the happiness of her growing and caring family.

Day 26. Psalms 70 - 72, Mishnah Pesachim 2

On November 26th 1978 Rosa died of cancer. It had been a mercifully short illness and she died in her sleep. For eighty two years she had lived a life devoted to truth and honesty, giving everything she had to others so they would benefit. Even after her death this would continue. Whilst she had lived with her daughter, Rosa had tried to save her small pension, only spending some of it on presents for her family. What was left she had wanted her daughter to keep for her two grandchildren.

And so it came to pass that the unimaginable came true, because thanks to those savings, the family were able to make their first trip to Israel for the *bar mitzvah* of her daughter's eldest son in 1981. It was a very moving experience in many ways, not least for the thought that, were it not for this feisty little refugee, who had struggled so hard and so valiantly, none of them would be standing by the *Kotel* that day. Three years later they repeated the trip for the younger brother's bar mitzvah.

These trips to Israel had a tremendous impact on both youngsters, and today, many years later, both of them point to their initial visits as watersheds in their Jewish growth. It is probably why both of them today are proud observant Jews, a living testimony to Rosa and all she stood for.

On May 31st 1996, almost 100 years to the day that Rosa was born, in a hospital in Jerusalem, Ariella Chava was born - the great-grandchild of Rosa Meth and the first Jew from her immediate family to be born in Israel.

This is a story that spans generations, wars, death and birth, and it is a testimony to one woman who still lives on in the lives of her grandchildren, and now four great grandchildren

I know this story well, because Rosa was my grandmother.

27 Absolute Morality

Steven Gaffin

Imagine that you are walking along in your local shopping precinct. Suddenly, to your delight, you see a brick. You pick it up and calmly smash it over the head of the old lady in front of you, grabbing her handbag as you flee. In the ensuing confusion, you slip into a local Marks and Spencer store where you steal some food, as well as a scarf and woolly hat as a disguise. Then you exit via a service door and make your way to a nearby car park where you hot-wire a car and flee the scene.

Do you have any problems with this pleasant suburban vignette? If so, why? Is it because you believe that mugging, shoplifting and theft are objectively and absolutely wrong? Or is it because you feel that society will break down if such things are tolerated?

It must be pointed out that we are not focusing here on questions of legality. We know that legality does not necessarily denote morality. For example, the Nuremberg Laws were legal in the sense that they were legally adopted by the Reichstag. Most fair-minded people though would not describe such legislation as 'moral', even if it may have been legal. Our discussion is, therefore, focused exclusively on morality.

It seems that there are two options. Either you adhere to the absoluteness of morality in which a source, outside of human intelligence has designed an eternal moral code for humanity. Or, as a relativist, you reject the existence of an objective morality in the world and thus, the notion of absolute good or evil. You can believe either of these but you cannot maintain both.

If a relativist stance is applied consistently, relativism could conceivably be a valid philosophical position, too. The same cannot be said of those who merge the two philosophies, claiming that *certain* things are absolute while others are discretionary. For example, many people believe that murder is an absolute evil, whilst at the same time asserting that keeping kosher is a matter of choice. But what source declares that murder is absolutely evil? If it is the Torah, then this is the same Torah which states that a Jew must keep kosher.

If one chooses which *mitzvot* of the Torah they want to keep and accept, then they cannot logically claim that murder, incest and paedophilia are absolutely wrong. They may feel that the aforementioned actions are distasteful and that they deplore those who do them. They might even go so far as to say that, in their view, society might be damaged or even endangered by such actions. However, since relativists reject the absolutist approach, they cannot absolutely condemn any action.

The following story illustrates the limitations of this quasi-relativist stance. A philosophy undergraduate once wrote an essay on absolute morality in which he argued there was no such thing. His lecturer returned it with a failing mark at the bottom. When the student challenged his teacher, saying that he had written a cogent defence of his position, the lecturer replied that although this was true, he felt like failing him, so he did. The student was outraged.

"That is totally unfair!" he ranted.

"Are you absolutely sure?" his professor asked. Seeing the seething student nodding, he continued, "If so, you do believe in absolutes after all!" The point was well taken. Most people will reject relativism when their backs are against the wall.

Nevertheless, some people are prepared to say, even in such circumstances, that there is no such thing as absolute morality. In other words, for them, no matter what the circumstances, each of us is morally autonomous. They might accept societal norms, but their own view is such that there are no absolutes other than the fact that there are no absolutes.

As previously noted, this is a plausible philosophical position. However, we need to examine the implications of such a view. Some years ago, Kevin Carter, a freelance photographer, took a photograph that launched the Ethiopian famine relief effort and won him the Pulitzer Prize. Three months after receiving it, Carter was found dead, killed by the exhaust fumes of his own truck. The note he left cited the criticism he had received for taking the photo. The image depicted a dying child crouching on the ground. Several metres away a vulture was perched, opportunistically awaiting the toddler's death. People accused the photographer of unparalleled callousness for doing nothing to aid the unfortunate child. So what would have been the correct course of action? Take the shot or help the victim? For the relativist there is no right answer. In a world without moral parameters it actually doesn't matter what action (or inaction) you take.

For the true relativist there can be no objective boundaries. Nothing is absolutely right and nothing is absolutely wrong. This effectively means that one can do what one likes at any given moment, which may be great, but what comes with it is that nothing has any ultimate meaning beyond the manufactured reasoning of the individual mind. In other words, whether you help the old lady across the road or wallop her with a brick, it doesn't really make a difference. Meaning or no meaning, the choice is yours. Judaism however tells us that there is an absolute morality of which God is the source. There *are* absolute moral choices to be made.

28 The Chosen People: An Often Misunderstood Idea

Aubrey Hersh

The Jewish nation is often referred to as "the Chosen People". Many people find this concept disturbing, since chosen-ness appears to set one group of people apart from the rest, designating them as superior. This strikes the modern mind as racist and seems uncomfortably close to the Nazi concept of a superior 'Aryan' nation. Given that the great passion of our time is equality for all, any discussion of what chosen-ness really means is lost in a storm of negative emotions.

In actual fact, when the Torah refers to the Jews as having been "chosen", it is not a claim of racial difference or superiority. How could it be? After all, our nation includes Germans, Russians, Arabs, Americans, Asians, etc. because Jews are as racially varied as there are races! All the same, the term "Chosen People" does denote a distinctiveness to those who are part of the Jewish nation.

Equality

Before analysing the Jewish idea of chosen-ness, let's first examine the flip-side of chosen-ness – equality. Western thinking promotes the idea that all people are equal. In fact the American Declaration of Independence states, "We declare all men to be created equal." But is this true? Are all people, in fact, equal?

As Rabbi Professor Dovid Gottlieb points out: "Clearly, in some respects, we are all the same. We are all born, we die, breathe, eat and sleep. Yet we vary considerably in *most* other areas: physical characteristics, intelligence, financial well-being, personality traits, education, etc... Furthermore just as individuals differ, so do nations. They are strong in certain areas and weak in others. The United States, for example, is consistently strong in technology and weak in fundamental theoretical science, whereas Germanic education has produced one-third of the Nobel prizes in science in this century."[1]

Given these differences, does a wholesale assertion of equality make any sense? We cannot philosophically oppose the existence of chosen-ness, based merely on the blind desire of *wanting* everyone to be equal. As such, when we refer to equality nowadays, we cannot and do not mean this descriptively but rather conceptually; namely that everyone should be treated fairly, without negative discrimination. This is a position which Judaism *wholeheartedly* endorses and promotes.

A Chosen Nation: Chosen by whom and why?

In ancient times, *Abraham* came to a belief in monotheism, and taught this concept to others. He was even willing to suffer persecution for his ideas, so much so, that after years of dedication forged in fire, God chose Abraham and his descendents to be the bearers of this monotheistic message.

In other words, as much as God chose the Jews, the Jews (via Abraham) chose God. In point of fact, the Torah tells us that this 'choosing' was not actually part of God's 'original plan.' Only after *Adam's* sin in the *Garden of Eden*, followed by the sins of the generation of the Flood and the *Tower of Babel*, did the elevated level on which Adam automatically related to God, disappear. Henceforth, it would have to be achieved through the individual choices of each member of mankind. Abraham made those choices. [2]

Five hundred years later at *Mount Sinai*, the opportunity presented itself once again for the entire world to share in this gift. However, the other nations of the world turned down this offer, leaving the Jewish people as the '*Am HaNivchar*' the Chosen People, since they were the only ones who accepted upon themselves the task of living a Torah way of life.

Nevertheless, even today, 3,000 years down the line, that

choice is still available to anyone who wishes to take it up. Regardless of race, creed and culture, Judaism will accept sincere converts from any background. Who is more central to Judaism, to Monarchy and to the messianic concept than *King David*? Who is more important to the Oral Law than *Rabbi Akiva*? Yet, both of them were descended from converts, as the *Talmud* clearly relates. Whereas, *Shemaya* and *Avtalyon*, two great leaders, and the teachers of the famous sage *Hillel*, were converts in their own right. For those willing to make the extra effort, the rewards are commensurate.

To draw an analogy, it is reasonable that an employee who agrees to work overtime, attend training seminars, and put themselves out for the company, should be entitled to certain privileges, particularly if each employee was, and is, offered the same opportunities.

Chosen-ness in Judaism although intrinsically due to past performance is still open to every member of the human race, without exception.

Chosen for what?

The essence of being chosen means undertaking the challenge and responsibility to influence the world – not by converting everyone to Judaism, but by living as a model community guided by Divine ethics and morals: to establish a culture devoted to God, and in doing so, be exposed to the possible scorn and, at times, hatred of other nations.

Ironically, this chosen-ness, rather than resulting in a smug sense of superiority, has left many Jews saying, "*It's too hard to be a Jew, to be chosen!!*"

Chosen-ness in Judaism is for the purpose of accomplishment. We are chosen to perform a role.

The consequences of chosen-ness

The natural corollary of being chosen for the assignment of bringing the Divine into the world is that our destiny has to enable us to carry this out. Thus, our history is different from that of all other nations. This is evident in two ways:

Firstly, our historical uniqueness is evident in our miraculous national survival. As Paul Johnson writes, "The Jews are the most tenacious people in history; Hebron is there to prove it. When the historian visits there today, he asks himself where are the Canaanites, the Edomites, the Babylonians, the Hellenes, the Romans, the Byzantines, the Franks, the Ottomans. They have vanished into time irrevocably... but the Jews are still in Hebron."[3]

It is further evident through our prominence. Our contribution to almost all societies amongst whom Jews have lived is disproportionate to our miniscule numbers. We don't make up even 1% of human race.[4] Yet as Mark Twain commented, "The Jew has contributed to literature, science, art, finance, medicine, and has done it with his hands tied behind him." He ends, in fact, by asking, "What is the secret of his immortality?"[5] Sociologically speaking, it is a fair question.

Even our enemies have spoken of our achievements. Hitler in Mein Kampf writes, "The Jews have inflicted two wounds on mankind – circumcision on its body and 'conscience' on its soul. They are Jewish inventions.... I free humanity from the shackles of the soul, from the degrading suffering caused by the false vision called conscience and ethics."

Chosen-ness in Judaism contains certain divine promises – both positive and negative – which can be clearly traced through the last 3,000 years of history.

Is Judaism racist?

Judaism believes that all of mankind was created in the image of God. In fact, the Talmud tells us we are all descended from one couple, and therefore the Torah begins not from the life of Abraham, but with the creation of Adam.

Moreover, Judaism has no missionaries because it believes that non-Jews can potentially achieve a share in the World to Come without converting, in accordance with their deeds. Indeed in Temple times, the Jewish nation would bring 70 sacrifices on *Succot* in order to pray for the welfare of the 70 nations of the world, acknowledging not only their existence but their individuality.

Furthermore, Judaism fully believes that other nations can be superior in many respects. Each nation has a God-given genius. Who can match the contribution of the ancient Greeks in design and architecture, of the Phoenicians in their genius for commerce and trade?

In conclusion

Our chosen-ness does not lessen our concern for, and duty toward, mankind. Nor does it interfere with the potential ability of other nations to create for themselves a place in the World to Come, and it certainly does not allow or excuse arrogant behavior toward others. However, it does demand of us to exhibit a stubborn tenacity in creating a yearning for, and contact with, God, so that the qualities of godliness can be brought into the world. This is a privileged and rewarding yet awesome undertaking, but it can be chosen by anyone prepared to make the necessary commitment should they so desire. Chosen to teach, to inspire... by personal and collective example.

Notes:
1 *The Informed Soul* – Artscroll publications p.112
2 The idea is developed further by Rabbi Shraga Simons
3 Paul Johnson: *History of the Jews* – p.4
4 World population figures: 6.4 billion. Jewish population figures: 14 million
5 Mark Twain: *Concerning the Jews* (1898)

29 Saving the World: A Kabbalistic View

Yaacov Haber

During the Six Day War, when bomb shelters were full and air raid sirens were blasting, many of the inhabitants of the Meah Shearim area of Jerusalem sat together in one bomb shelter. Among them was the great Rosh Yeshiva of Mir, HaRav Chaim Shmuelevitz of blessed memory. Together, people said Tehillim and prayed that they should not be harmed and that Jerusalem should be liberated. Amongst them was a woman who was known to all. She had been divorced and had gone through a great deal of agony from her ex-husband. She had spent years in pain over matrimonial issues. Suddenly the woman blurted out and said to God, "I forgive my husband for all the pain he has caused me. Just let us come out of this alive." Rav Chaim turned to his students and said, "If we leave this shelter unharmed and, in fact, if Israel wins the war, I believe it is in the merit of this woman."

The world was created not just once, but continues to be created by God on an ongoing basis. Think about creation as a light bulb – where the energy must flow through the filaments constantly. The moment the switch is shut off, light ceases to shine. God did not create the world and walk away; He keeps his finger on the button, creating and recreating the world every millisecond.

The 'juice' of creation goes through four stages before it reaches the level of creation that we can touch and feel. Kabbalistic literature refers to this as "*ABYA*" which stands for *Atzilut Briya Yitzirah and Assiyah*. The creative process starts off as a concept of God and begins in Atzilut, the highest spiritual level, closest to God. It then takes some form in the worlds of Briya and Yitzirah and is finally actualised in the world we know, the world of Assiyah, the world of actualisation. Like a generator into which the world is plugged, the energy flows through these four stages second by second.

A miracle, according to this understanding, is not a change in nature but simply different ingredients placed into the circuit at the source. When so called "good" happens in the world this is because there is good energy coming through the pipeline; when seemingly bad things take place the energy coming through the conduit is negative.

What is the raw material of the energy that is constantly creating the world? The Torah tells us that the source of this energy is the deeds of people. It starts with the deeds of human beings living in the world of Assiyah.

Picture the rain cycle:
Water is on the earth, the water evaporates and forms a cloud, and the cloud then bursts and replenishes the world with water. When we pollute the water on Earth it returns to us in the form of acid rain. A polluted liquid evaporates and descends in an unhealthy form, not necessarily where it went up. Pollution can go up in New York and come down in Canada, Africa or in Asia.

So too, our actions are the positive or negative energy of creation. If a peace treaty is signed in Sudan, it might be because of a random act of kindness in Asia. If civil war breaks out in Rwanda, it might be because of an act of violence that takes place In New York.

The good and bad we do form the raw material for the energy that then creates and recreates the world every second.

In a small town in Poland some young students asked their sagacious teacher the Chafetz Chaim whether it would be appropriate for them to contribute to the betterment of the world by leaving the yeshiva and joining the underground or pursuing some other involvement in world issues.

The Chafetz Chaim replied with a legendary statement, "The Torah which we study and the acts of kindness that we do in our small unknown town of Radin are directly affecting the discussions taking place at this moment in the British parliament."

One of the most trying epochs in the history of the Jewish people took place in the year 3828 – 68 C.E. The Jews lived in the land of Israel. Jerusalem was our religious centre. The Temple of Jerusalem stood gloriously and a renaissance of scholarship was underway.

However, the Roman Empire was growing daily and the dreadful time had come when the Roman Empire decided to conquer Jerusalem. The Jews in Israel were in a state of shock and fear. A group known as Beryonim, militant nationalists, decided to fight till the bitter end. The Rabbinic leadership felt that the right thing to do was to make peace with the Romans. The Beryonim went so far as to threaten the lives of some of the leading Rabbinic figures; Rabbi Yochanon Ben Zakai, had to be smuggled out of Jerusalem in a coffin in order to negotiate with the Roman Emperor Vespasian. The internal strife and battles escalated. We no longer felt a unity amongst our people. We no longer enjoyed brotherhood. The Talmud labeled this culture as *Sinat Chinam* the 'causeless hate' generation. In the year 70 CE the Temple was destroyed by the Romans.

The Talmud tells us that in fact it wasn't the Romans that destroyed the Temple but our infighting and hate. According to the teaching of the *Nefesh Hachaim*, it was the negative energy that we circulated into the ongoing creative process, *Sinat Chinam*, that positioned the Temple for destruction. In the words of the Talmud *"kimcha tachun tochanta"* the flour was already ground. By the time the Romans came to destroy the Temple in Jerusalem it was so devoid of its positive energy that it was a pushover, a straw house. Such is the power of *Sinat Chinam*.

We can become sensitive to the energy we evaporate into the creative process. A good word, a bit of causeless love and a little forgiveness may just save the world.

30 How Can 'Religious People' Fail in Their Moral Conduct?

Danny Kirsch

Is there a distinction between religious Jews committing crimes such as fraud, and religious Jews breaking the laws of *Shabbat* and *Kashrut*?

The Torah undeniably prohibits all of the above, and the prophets were repeatedly instructed to admonish those who simply went through the motions of looking 'religious' but whose moral behaviour was lacking. Clearly, therefore, a person identifying themselves as a 'religious' Jew is committing themselves to living by Torah law. Merely appearing to be 'religious', or using religious ritual as a veneer whilst reneging on the Torah's laws, is unacceptable within Judaism.

The Torah tells us that when Moses came down from *Mount Sinai* he brought down the Ten Commandments inscribed in stone. Unlike the classical representations of these tablets, the description in the Torah makes it quite clear that the tablets were actually two separate pieces of stone. The first tablet contained commandments one to five which encapsulated our relationship with God. The second tablet contained commandments six to ten, defining our relationship with mankind. Yet, when Moses witnessed the people worshipping the *Golden Calf* at the foot of *Mount Sinai*, thereby negating their relationship with God, he smashed *both* tablets in front of them.

Many Torah commentators inquire as to why the second tablet needed to be destroyed, since the commandments contained therein (those legislating social relationships) had not been compromised. The answer is that it is imperative that there be a moral consistency in relationships, whether between man and God or between man and man. The Jewish people cannot be guilty of moral schizophrenia. Therefore, Judaism views abuse and fraud, in the same way as it views the abrogation of Shabbat and circumcision.

As such, it's not the Torah that produces fraudulent people but rather fraudulent people who don't *allow* the Torah to affect them; Judaism isn't to blame, the individual Jew is. Individuals are culpable because the Torah expects them to be honest and overcome their frailties and temptations.

Moreover, so called 'religious' people who behave inconsistently, bring about a *chillul Hashem* – desecration of God's name. As the *Talmud* explains, if someone studies Bible but is dishonest in business and disrespectful in his dealings with people, what do people say about him: "Woe to him who studies Torah... this man studies the Torah, look how corrupt are his deeds, how ugly are his ways." [1]

However, before accusing people of wrongdoing it *is* important to ascertain that the misdeed was actually committed. Simply reading about it in the newspaper or hearing about it third hand is insufficient. Judaism demands factual evidence before making any judgments. Furthermore, Jewish laws obligates one to give people the benefit of the doubt, before weighing in against them; this isn't just an act of piety but an actual Biblical obligation. [2]

The *Rebbe* of Kotzk put it all together succinctly, by quoting a verse from the Torah, "Do not deceive your fellow man," [3] adding, "not to deceive another person is mandated by law. However the pious person – the *truly* religious Jew – also refrains from deceiving himself."

Notes:
1 Yoma 86a
2 Leviticus 19:15
3 Leviticus 25: 17

31 Treatment of Animals

Gavin Broder

On a number of occasions my children have asked (or perhaps begged) to own a pet. The usual response has been, "Who will look after it, who will feed it, who will clean up the mess it makes?"

In reality however, there are far more responsibilities that a person has towards their animals. Judaism addresses these duties and the sensitivity that a person has to show. Let us examine a few of these.

In describing the reward that the Jewish people will receive for adhering to the commandments, God promises, "I will give grass in your fields for your animals, and you will eat and be satisfied."[1] The *Talmud* observes that the verse places the feeding of the animals before that of man and deduces that it is forbidden for a person to partake of food unless he has first fed his animals.[2] The force of this law is incorporated in the *Shulchan Aruch*[3] in a fascinating way. The law discusses the prohibition of speaking between saying the blessing over bread and eating the bread, and states, "If a person interrupts between saying the blessing and eating the bread, he needs to repeat the blessing, *unless* what he says is related to the meal." Included in 'something related to the meal' is if he says, "Give food to the animals." We therefore see, the importance that is placed on feeding one's animals.[4]

There are two further instances where the Torah places demands upon us regarding animals and food:

In Deuteronomy it states, "Do not muzzle an ox when it is treading grain."[5] That is, you may not deprive an animal of eating food while it works in the field, and, "Do not plough with an ox and a donkey together."[6] This law applies to any two species of animals and includes all types of work e.g. pulling a wagon.[7] *Sefer HaChinuch* explains that the underlying reason for this prohibition is that "various species of animals have great anxiety when placed with others not of their own kind, and all the more so when forced to work together".[8]

What transpires from the above is that apart from the obligation to feed an animal there is an obligation to be conscious of the 'feelings' of animals.

It almost goes without saying that we are further commanded not to cause unnecessary pain to animals. We read in the Bible about the prohibition of overloading a beast of burden. If one sees such an animal being crushed under the weight that it is forced to carry, one must assist in unloading the burden from that animal. This is true even if the owner of that animal is personally unworthy of your help in that matter. The animal is not made to suffer because of the bad behaviour of its owner. And in a famous response (rabbinical reply to a legal question), the eighteenth century scholar and the rabbi of Prague, Rabbi Yechezkel Landau, forbids hunting animals or birds for sport. In addition to the Torah prohibition of not causing pain to an animal, we are also obliged to show gratitude to them!

Furthermore, the Torah in requiring us to treat animals in a well-defined manner, is at the same time imbuing within us certain character traits that will reflect on the way that we treat fellow human beings. There is a well known *Midrash* that relates, that once while Moses was tending the sheep of Jethro, a kid goat ran away. Moses ran after it until he found it drinking at a pool of water. He realised that the kid had run away because it was thirsty and now deduced that it must also be tired. He promptly carried it on his shoulder and returned. God, seeing this said, "You are compassionate in leading flocks belonging to mortals; I swear you will similarly shepherd my flock, Israel".[9] It was this quality of caring about a helpless animal that made God decide that Moses should become the leader of the Jewish people.

It is altogether apparent, therefore, that long before animal welfare organisations came into being, Judaism showed high regard for the way that we are expected to treat animals. It should be further understood that when Judaism sanctioned *Shechitah*, the killing of animals for consumption, it did so with these 'codes of conduct' in mind.

Like all moral rights though, these have to be judged in perspective, balanced with other moral rights and with proper standards. Mankind may use animals to further human work and health and to create a better society. The Torah states that this privilege to use animals for human benefit was granted to mankind by God Himself. Without rhesus monkeys there would have been no polio vaccine. Artificial limbs, organ transplants, miracle drugs and revolutionary surgical procedures all have been a fabulous boon to mankind, especially over the past decades of breathtaking medical progress. In God's world, animal rights are relative and not absolute, secondary to human progress and health. Animal species are not to be made extinct in order to produce exotic purses, but the use of animals to save and improve human lives is essential and permissible.[10] It is part of man's pact with nature and its Creator.

Notes:

1 Deuteronomy 11:15
2 Berachot 40b, Gittin 62a
3 Orach Chaim 167:6
4 Magen Avraham 18
5 Deuteronomy 25:4
6 Deuteronomy 22:10
7 Mishnah Kilayim 8:2
8 Mitzvah 550
9 Shemot – Parshat Bo
10 Rabbi Berel Wein: *Living Jewish* pg 279

32 Why Should I Marry?

Dr Julian Shindler

Figures from the Office of National Statistics indicate that, over the past decade or so, more people have chosen not to marry. This trend, compounded with the rise in assimilation, out-marriage, and marrying later in life, is bad news for the demography of the Jewish community.

Getting married for the wrong reasons often proves a recipe for disaster. But there are many people who seem to opt out of marriage because of social trends driven by the media. If it is deemed 'un-cool' to be married, why bother? If remaining single improves career prospects, what advantages are secured by bucking the trend?

Central to this mode of thinking is the assumption that, if one is unencumbered by the bonds of marriage then personal fulfillment and happiness is assured. Marriage is seen as imposing responsibilities towards another person which limit the individual. By remaining single, one can do what one likes, when one likes.

Today's secular society promotes sexual license, encouraging promiscuity. A track record of sexual encounters may provide moments of recreational 'fun', but is exploitative of others and is unlikely to result in lasting happiness because it is essentially self-serving and narcissistic.

In contrast, the Hebrew word for love (*ahavah*) is derived from a root that means 'giving.' Jewish marriage is characterised by a relationship of mutual respect and giving in which both parties can achieve personal growth. The marital home is the space in which husband and wife complement each other and fulfill themselves. In fact, when a Jewish child is named we pray that he should grow to merit the *chuppah* and *ma'asim tovim* (good deeds). Marriage is thus seen as sanctified by God and an ideal to which to aspire.

Jewish marriage, like most other worthwhile pursuits, makes demands on the husband and the wife, yet the potential rewards are immense. Together they can discover happiness that is not merely of a transient nature. The laws of marital intimacy, with their cycle of self-restraint, yearning, anticipation and fulfillment help sustain the intensity of the physical side of their relationship whilst making space for developing a sense of companionship. If the union is fortunate to be blessed with the arrival of children, the couple will experience both the joy and the challenge of raising the next generation of Jews.

Judaism accepts the possibility that marriages can go wrong and provides a mechanism for divorce. However, the *Talmud* records that when this occurs, the altar in the Temple metaphorically sheds tears. By contrast, the metaphor used to describe the situation in which a couple sets up a home steeped in Jewish practice and values, refers to the rebuilding of Jerusalem.

Despite all the social experimentation of the last century marriage has proved to be the best framework for a man and a woman to find lasting meaning and fulfillment in life. This whole enterprise of marriage and family has been the cornerstone on which the survival of our people has depended. Given the opportunity, we should choose to opt in, not out.

33 The Torah That Journeyed From the Depths to the Heavens

Michael Laitner

A eulogy is normally only said for a person. Eulogies concentrate on what people have achieved. But this story tells the remarkable history of a *Sefer Torah*, which was used and cherished for many years in many lands before finally disappearing in front of the whole world.

It is the chronicle of a Sefer Torah that made its first appearance in a concentration camp – the very depths of human cruelty – and its last appearance in the soaring height of human ingenuity – a space shuttle. This Sefer Torah deserves its own kind of eulogy. Its tale must be told.

Here follows the account of Debbi Wigoren, a Washington Post reporter, who, incidentally, is not Jewish:

The *Bar Mitzvah* took place before dawn on a Monday in March, 1944, inside a barracks at the Bergen-Belsen concentration camp.

Those men who were strong enough covered the windows and doors with blankets and stood watch to make sure that no SS guards were coming.

Four candles, scrounged from somewhere, gave off enough flickering light for Rabbi Samuel Dasberg to unfurl this tiny Sefer Torah – the five books of Moses, handwritten by a scribe, on a parchment scroll that was just four and a half inches tall.

Thirteen year old Joachim Joseph chanted the blessings just as the rabbi had taught him, and then he chanted aloud from the ancient scroll in the singsong Hebrew melody that has been passed down for hundreds of years.

"There were people listening in the beds all around," Joachim Joseph, who is now a 71 year old Israeli physicist, recalls, describing the narrow triple decker bunks where the Jewish men and boys slept. "Afterwards everybody congratulated me. Somebody fished out a piece of a chocolate bar that he had been saving and gave it to me. And somebody else fished out a deck of playing cards for me too. Everybody told me, "now you are a Bar Mitzvah, now you are an adult. We are so very proud of you. Mazel tov!" And I felt very good.

"And then everything was quickly taken down, and we went out to roll call."

Rabbi Dasberg also gave Joseph a gift that day. He gave him the miniature Torah scroll that they had used, covered in a red velvet wrapper and tucked into a small green box.

He said: "This little Sefer Torah is yours to keep now, because I am pretty sure that I will not get out of this place alive, but maybe you will." "And you know how children are," Joachim Joseph said when the Washington Post interviewed him by long distance phone. "At first, I didn't want to take it, but he insisted. He convinced me. And the condition was I had to promise that if I ever got out of there, that I must tell the story, the story of my Bar Mitzvah."

The story of Joachim Joseph and that Sefer Torah was told to the world on January 21st, when Ilan Ramon, the first Israeli astronaut, held the scroll aloft during a live teleconference from aboard the space shuttle Columbia.

"This Torah scroll was given by a rabbi to a young, scared, thin, thirteen year old boy in Bergen-Belsen," Ramon said from inside the space shuttle. "It represents more than anything the ability of the Jewish people to survive. It represents their ability to go from black days, from periods of darkness, to reach periods of hope and faith in the future."

And then, 11 days after that interview, spaceship Columbia disintegrated on its way back down to earth, and Ilan Ramon and the other members of that crew were killed.

Not all of the experiments and projects that this mission

was supposed to accomplish were successful. Many of those experiments perished with them. The results of some of them were sent back down to earth before the Columbia crashed and so they were not lost. But I think that the Sefer Torah fulfilled its mission more thoroughly than any of the other objects aboard that spaceship.

One day a few years ago, Ilan Ramon was visiting the home of Joachim Joseph in Tel Aviv. He noticed this miniature Sefer Torah on a shelf in Joseph's study and he asked him what it was. Dr. Joseph, who is now a well known physicist in Israel, explained to him that this Sefer Torah was given to him, in Bergen-Belsen, on the day of his bar mitzvah.

He explained that he was born in Berlin and raised in Amsterdam. The young Joseph had watched with interest as older boys in his neighbourhood celebrated their bar mitzvahs. His father, a lawyer, was not particularly religious, but several of his uncles were, and they would sometimes take him with him when they went to synagogue.

Joachim Joseph was not particularly devoted to Jewish rituals, but he did look forward to experiencing the excitement of becoming a Bar Mitzvah.

And then the Nazis came.

The family was sent to a Dutch prison camp called Westerbork, late in 1942. A year later, the Josephs were brought to Bergen-Belsen, the concentration camp in the Lower Saxony region of Germany, where sixty thousand people died, including their compatriot, Anne Frank.

Joachim and his younger brother ended up in a barracks, with Rabbi Dasberg, the former Chief Rabbi of the Netherlands. When Rabbi Dasberg heard that Joachim Joseph was becoming 13 years old, the age of bar mitzvah, he asked if he could teach him. They studied together secretly at night.

"We were still in a good enough condition that we could entertain the thought of doing such a thing," Dr. Joseph remembers. But a couple of months later, Rabbi Dasberg disappeared from his barracks. He died on February 24th, 1945, just a few months before British troops liberated the camp.

Joachim Joseph used rags to wrap the green box that held the Torah, and he hid it deep down at the bottom of his backpack. It stayed there, undetected, as conditions in the camp grew worse and worse.

Freedom came out of the blue. In February 1945, a maternal uncle who had fought for the French Resistance and then escaped to Switzerland, secured fake passports for Joachim and his family from several Latin American countries, something that was very rare so late in the war. The brothers and their parents, emaciated and near death, were reunited and put on a train, with captured foreign nationals whom the Germans hoped to exchange for their own POWs. Months later, the family sailed on a British military ship to Palestine, part of a generation of refugees who were determined to build a Jewish state.

In 1951, Joachim Joseph published the story of his clandestine Bar Mitzvah in the *Jerusalem Post*. He hated talking about his life in the concentration camps, and so he did not want to write the article, but his father, who remembered the promise his son had made to Rabbi Dasberg, insisted.

For the next four decades, Joseph said almost nothing about his experiences during the war. He wanted to stop the nightmares he kept having, and he wanted to move on.

"I screwed it down, deep down," he says. "I did my best to forget about it."

He studied atmospheric physics, and got a doctorate from UCLA in 1966. He pioneered experiments in how dust particles in the atmosphere affect the climate. And that is how he came to meet Ilan Ramon.

A few months later, Ramon called from Houston and asked him for permission to take the Sefer Torah along with him when he went up into space.

"I'm not sorry that it is gone," he says. "It did what it, perhaps, was destined to do."

This Sefer Torah was not just a link in the chains of Jewish generations, but a personal testament to the life of its extraordinary owner, a microcosm of the cataclysmic events in

Jewish history over the last 65 years. It traveled from the bustling and vibrant Jewish quarter of Amsterdam, to the horrors of a concentration camp, through the crossroads of the displaced persons camps, and finally to the rebuilt Jewish commonwealth in the State of Israel, formed in 1948, barely three years after the end of World War Two.

Who knows what the Sefer Torah was 'destined' to do? Did Rabbi Dasberg, even as he courageously tutored his pupil in the concentration camp, even as he optimistically and heroically bore the torch of Jewish continuity? Did he ever imagine that his student would become a famous Israeli physicist, and that the Sefer Torah and its story would be displayed before millions of television viewers, by an astronaut, as it went into space?

When Rabbi Dasberg bequeathed the Sefer Torah to his brave young pupil, he made him promise that if his pupil would survive the killing fields of the concentration camps, he would tell the story of this Sefer Torah. Could he have ever envisaged that his pupil would keep this promise so tenaciously and so faithfully, in front of the watching eyes of the world?

For this reason alone, this Sefer Torah, which stayed with its owner as he stayed with it, deserves a eulogy.

This Sefer Torah reminds us of another Sefer Torah that went up in flames. On *Yom Kippur*, we read the story of the 10 famous Rabbis who were martyred by the Romans. One of them, Rabbi Chanina ben Teradyon, was brought to the stake for burning, wrapped in a Sefer Torah. As the flames began to lick at the parchment, the rabbi's students, distraught at the agony of their teacher, approached him and asked "What do you see?" Their teacher replied, "I see the scrolls burning, and the letters flying away". When those words left his lips, his soul passed on.

The Torah Scroll itself may have burnt, but its letters flew straight up to heaven, never to be destroyed. So too, the words of the Torah, and the Jewish people have survived.

The tiny Sefer Torah, passed by a remarkable rabbi, Rabbi

Dasberg, to a dedicated, brave and faithful student, Dr Joseph, to a heroic astronaut, Ilan Ramon, accompanied the Jewish people through some of its most momentous journeys, from lows to highs, and even to outer space. It too went up in smoke, alongside some brave and much mourned astronauts. But, its story goes on, just like the letters of Rabbi Chanina ben Teradyon's Sefer Torah. May the Sefer Torah, and the courage of its keepers, never be forgotten.

Excerpts reprinted with permission from the
Washington Post ©2003

34 The Wonder of the State of Israel

James Kennard

Over 2,400 years ago, Nebuchadnezzar's armies swept through the Jewish kingdom and razed Jerusalem to the ground. Jews were exiled throughout the Babylonian empire, and the Jewish people was destined to disappear – sharing the fate of other small conquered nations who either died out or assimilated.

But it was not to be. The Jewish nation survived exile and seventy years later, re-established a presence in Israel, rebuilding their Temple and re-creating Jewish life. Then in 70 CE, Roman legions occupied Jerusalem, destroyed the Temple and all vestiges of Jewish sovereignty, and massacred or enslaved one third of the Jewish nation.

Again, with the demise of the Jewish State, the demise of the Jewish people seemed to be close at hand, especially after the brutal suppression of the last remnants of Jewish nationalism – the Bar Kochba rebellion – in 135 CE. But again, the Jewish people defied the rules of history and, after two millennia of wanderings and much suffering, returned home.

Thus in 1948, a nation, that had just risen from the ashes of the concentration camps, returned to the land which was promised to the Patriarchs and the land from which it had been twice exiled, and there re-established its own independence. For a nation to return to its land once is unprecedented in human history. For it to happen twice is surely miraculous.

Today, 56 more years have passed, and most Jews cannot recall a time when there was no State of Israel. It is therefore sometimes hard to appreciate the miraculous nature of the transformation of the Jewish people that took place at the moment of Israel's independence – the transformation of the dispossessed of the Diaspora, to the autonomy that we enjoy today.

During recent decades we have seen the reality of the ingathering of the exiles, as foretold by the prophets. The vast communities of the Jewish Diaspora of North Africa, the Arab world and most recently the former Soviet Union have returned to Israel, as well as large numbers from every continent. Jews have made *aliyah* to Israel in order to build new lives in their homeland, but also to escape anti-semitism and persecution. Because of the existence of the State of Israel, Jews all over the world have a sheltered place of refuge – another unprecedented phase in the last millennia of Jewish history.

Israel's military achievements represent another miracle, revealing yet again the Hand of God, in our fortunes. Today, when Israel is acknowledged to be a strong country, it is easy to forget how in 1948 and again in 1967, it was assumed that the small Israeli Defence Forces would easily be overwhelmed by the vastly superior force of numerous Arab armies, leading to the State being stillborn in 1948, or destroyed in 1967. In each case, it was not to be, and Israel has survived not only those wars, but the ongoing state of belligerency and terrorist attacks.

A consequence of the re-establishment of the Jewish State has been the worldwide restoration of Jewish pride and a re-connection to Jewish heritage. In the wake of Israel's independence and subsequent victories, Jews around the world have stood up as proud members of their people. Especially after the Six-Day War in 1967, *kippot* were worn in public in a way that would have been unthinkable beforehand. That victory also sparked the re-awakening of Soviet Jewry, when thousands were prepared to risk persecution in order to seek out their Jewish heritage and to attempt to return to their homeland.

The *Ba'al Teshuva* movement – encouraging Jews to return to their religious roots and to Torah learning – was another unexpected by-product of this renewed sense of Jewish identity. Indeed it is in Israel, and because of Israel, that Torah is being learnt by more students than ever before in history.

Yet another reality that we too often take for granted, is the success of the State of Israel in creating a modern industrial state. Whilst its neighbours, despite their vast oil riches, remain underdeveloped in many respects, Israel's pioneers literally "made the desert bloom"; built towns and villages where previously there was wilderness or swamp; and created many industries. In fact as early as 1936, the British government – in the form of the Peel Commission – acknowledged that "much of the land now carrying orange groves was sand dunes or swamp and uncultivated when it was purchased."

In recent decades, Israel has become a world leader in hi-tech fields such as software engineering and processor manufacture. Israel has a highly educated population, including communities whose parents immigrated from societies where literacy, let alone university education, was rare. With less than 1/1000th of the world's population, Israel can make claim to having the highest ratio of university degrees to the population in the world, and to producing more scientific papers per capita than any other nation by a large margin. Israel is also relative to its population and size, the largest immigrant-absorbing nation on earth.

Too often we let problems of security and diplomacy – and our hopes and prayers for Israel to reach a state of perfection – obscure these tremendous achievements.

In his seminal work "Kol Dodi Dofek" – "the voice of my beloved is knocking", *Rav Joseph Dov Soloveitchik* describes the image from the Song of Songs[1] of one being awoken by the sound of one's beloved knocking at the door but not rising quickly enough to open the door. This, he presents as a parable to show how we should be listening, in our own times, to the sound of God knocking on our door.

We are privileged to live in a generation when God is giving many such 'knocks' – of which the loudest are the return of millions of Jews to their geographical and spiritual roots and the transformation of the Jew from a wretched wanderer to one living proud and upright in their own land.

When we consider the miraculous nature of the State of Israel perhaps we should listen for the sound of God knocking on our door. We may even want to answer the knocking...

Notes:

1 Song of Songs 5:3

35 Keeping the Flame Alive

Chief Rabbi Dr Jonathan Sacks

The story of Jewish continuity is a mystery. It is so today as the century of the Holocaust and the rebirth of Israel nears its close. It was so from the beginning, from the days of *Abraham* and *Sarah*.

It is as if a certain message were woven into our being from the very outset. To move from one generation of Jews to the next requires a miracle: a series of miracles. Nature is against it. Prediction rules otherwise. At times, even Heaven itself seems to conspire against it. And yet we are Jews today because of miracles.

Imagine trying to trace your family tree back beyond *bubbe* and *zeida* to their grandparents, and theirs. In the family chronicles of each Jew today, in the strange, tortuous, tangled path between Abraham and Sarah and us, is a succession of miracles that challenges belief. Somehow our ancestors survived the destructions and the exiles, the Crusades and the Blood Libels, the forced conversions and the Inquisitions, the persecutions and pogroms; survived, by accident or destiny, the Final Solution and the gas chambers. Somehow our parents and their parents and all the generations before them lived through hopelessness and despair, the wanderings and sufferings and against prediction and logic brought new generations of Jewish children into the world. There has been nothing like it in the history of humanity. Can we, dare we, be the last?

Today, we are losing our children. For three generations we were preoccupied with other things. Nor were they small matters. They touched on the very existence of Jews in the modern world. We could be forgiven for neglecting the

Jewishness of our children. There were other matters to attend to first. There was integration. There was survival. Not since the days of destruction of the Second Temple nineteen centuries ago has the Jewish people faced such dislocation, such collective trauma.

But that has passed. Today we face a situation that Jews have only rarely faced before in their four thousand year history: the challenge of creating a Jewish life in conditions of freedom and equality in the Diaspora and sovereignty in our own land, the land of Israel. That was always the ultimate challenge, and it reverberates throughout the lines of Jewish destiny like the unanswered question it is. We survived slavery. Can we survive freedom? We survived suffering. Can we survive security? We survived exile. Can we survive homecoming?

We will do none of these things unless, at long last, we put our children and their Jewish needs first. The Bible provides us with only one answer to the question which has puzzled Jew and non-Jew alike. Why Abraham? Why Israel? Why the Jewish people? Abraham, says the Bible, was chosen "so that he will direct his children and his household after him to keep the way of the Lord by doing what is right and just." Abraham was chosen not for himself but for his children and for what he would create in them: a way of life that they would value and continue to pass on. They would be a link in a chain of eternity.

Not all of us can have children. But each of us can do something to ensure that the Jewish people continues. We can make it possible for every Jewish child to experience, learn about and live the heritage which earned the admiration, and changed the civilisation, of the world. What we most need now to learn is not something new but the oldest Jewish instinct of all: a concern that something infinitely precious should live on through us into the next generation.

Let us not treat the future lightly. When God promised Abraham that his reward would be very great, he replied, "O Lord God, what will you give me if I remain childless?" That is the question eternity asks us. What will our lives and the lives of our ancestors mean if they are not lent immortality by our continuity, by our bringing it about that we have Jewish grandchildren? If we would only remember the many miracles it took to bring us to this hour, we would willingly do the many things needed to be done to bring the next generation into being, and the next. Jewish continuity is the greatest gift we can bring to the future and the past.

36 Death with Dignity

Chaim Rapoport

The first verse in the Torah to record the prohibition against homicide may be rendered as follows: "I will claim retribution for your bloodshed… from the hand of man – from the hand of the man who is his brother – I will claim retribution for having taken the life of another man".[1]

This passage is somewhat verbose, even awkward. Why is it necessary for the Torah to reiterate and state "from the hand of the man who is his brother"? Is there any reason to assume that 'fratricide' is less heinous a crime than 'homicide' for which reason the Torah had to state explicitly that killing a brother is equally forbidden?

Rabbi Yaakov Tzevi Mecklenberg, a 19th century Torah scholar, explains that the nuances of this verse were designed so as to condemn 'mercy killing'.

There are, he says, two types of murder. Ordinarily murder is motivated by anger, hatred and even sadism. Yet there are times when the desire to terminate someone's life may be borne out of a feeling of love and brotherhood. When a person one loves seems to have lost the capacity to enjoy life's blessings, perhaps life has become so painful that the person wants to die, one may be tempted to oblige them and bring a swift end to their suffering. One may have erroneously assumed that the Torah forbids only such homicide that is driven by animosity. The Torah therefore states that even when committed by a "man who is his brother" homicide contravenes God's will. Thus the condemnation of euthanasia is rooted in the very first biblical passage that forbids the taking of a human life.

What is the philosophical basis for the Torah's ban on euthanasia?

Some secular ethicists condemn euthanasia because of the 'slippery slope syndrome'. Their argument is: If we were to allow 'mercy killing', it will inevitably lead to 'killing' without mercy, therefore we are compelled to maintain a blanket prohibition on all types of killing. Accordingly euthanasia is truly an aspiration, albeit one that cannot be implemented, out of fear that the system may be abused.

Judaism, however, objects to euthanasia on absolute principle.

Some theologians have argued that from a religious perspective there is no such thing as a life not worth living, for whether we appreciate it or not, life is always a 'blessing'. Accordingly euthanasia is not only a crime, it represents a serious blemish in faith. Divine-given life is always better than death; to dispute this borders on blasphemy.

Yet this doctrine is arguably contradicted by the teaching of classical Rabbinic sources who clearly recognise that sometimes death may indeed be considered preferable to life.

Based on an episode related in the *Gemarah*[2], Rabbi Nissim Gerondi (14th Century) states that if a patient is suffering from a terminal illness and is undergoing great suffering it is appropriate to pray on his behalf that he die![3]

Clearly it is not considered audacious, let alone a symptom of faith deficiency, to ask God to put an end to the life of a suffering patient. The fact that one ought to pray to God and ask Him to hasten the death of a fellow Jew demonstrates that, in certain circumstances, such a death may indeed be a blessing. So why do we not practice what we pray for?

It is written in Psalms: "The earth and all therein is the Lord's; the world and all its inhabitants."[4] A crucial distinction should be made between the 'world' and its 'inhabitants'. Although God reserves the ultimate rights to all of our worldly assets, so long as they are in our possession we may do with them as we please. We can choose to sell or give away our belongings, and in some circumstances, even destroy them but the human 'inhabitants' of the world are essentially different. God never granted us ownership of our bodies and lives. He entrusted each person with the care and preservation of his body and its life. Man is not the 'owner' of his life he is merely a 'custodian'. As such he is granted certain privileges and prerogatives in relation to his 'self', but he has no right whatsoever to inflict damage upon his body or, worse still, to terminate its very life.

Only the Author and Owner of life has the right to bring it to an end. It is for this reason that the Torah prohibits suicide even when a patient is experiencing intense and prolonged pain as a result of an incurable disease. And it is based on the same principle that Judaism condemns 'mercy killing'. Euthanasia may therefore be described as the ultimate intrusion into God's domain.

As Rabbi Yechiel Michel Epstein (19th Century) in his *Aruch HaShulchan* writes, "although we see him suffering greatly in dying so that death is good for him, we are nevertheless forbidden to do anything to hasten his death" for he "belongs to the Holy One, Blessed by He, and such is His exalted will."[6]

In this remarkable statement Rabbi Epstein acknowledges that sometimes "death is good"(!) but asserts, nonetheless, that the patient – and by the same token anyone else he may wish to empower – has no licence regarding his life and soul. Life is God's possession and for the human being to play the role of owner amounts to usurpation of the divine life – hardly a dignified way to leave this world.

Notes:

1 Genesis 9:5

2 Ketubot 104a

3 This teaching should not be considered in isolation. It must be balanced with another axiom of our sages: "Even if a sharp sword is placed on a person's neck, he should not refrain from praying for merciful salvation" (Berachot 10a). Judaism is an optimistic faith and it is such a statement that has enabled us – both collective and individually – to see the light at the end of many a dark tunnel, and persevere with courage and confidence, despite all 'doomsday' prophets and prognosis. But we are able to see the wood and the trees. Whilst we always hope

and pray for recovery, we recognise that He who answers prayers sometimes says 'no'. Our affirmation of God's sovereignty and omniscience also dictates that we accept that sometimes – for reasons beyond our comprehension – the Almighty does allow people to endure untold suffering. These convictions empower us to beseech God to bring a miraculous cure to a terminally ill patient and, at the same time, pray that if he in the event that that the "sharp sword" is not destined to be removed from the 'neck', let the patient suffer no more and let him find solace in the world of divine bliss.

4 Psalms 24:1
5 Psalms 115:16
6 Yoreh Deah 339:1

37 Brit Milah: Completion Through Incompleteness

Mordechai Ginsbury

"On the eighth day the flesh of his (a new-born Jewish male's) foreskin shall be circumcised."[1] The *Midrash*[2] comments on this verse: "Turnus Rufus, a Roman emperor, posed two questions to *Rabbi Akiva*. 'Whose deeds are more noble, those of God or humans?' Rabbi Akiva answered that human deeds are nobler. Turnus Rufus also asked, 'why do Jews practice *Brit Milah*?' Rabbi Akiva produced some sheaves of wheat and loaves of bread and emphasised the attractiveness of the finished loaves over the raw sheaves. Turnus Rufus responded, 'surely if God wants male circumcision, why are boys not born circumcised?' Rabbi Akiva replied that the entire purpose of the commandments given to the Jewish people is to refine and elevate them through their actions."

The 18th century commentator *Ohr HaChayim* finds this dialogue hard to understand. Why does the lengthy process of transforming wheat into bread explain or justify circumcision? If God created the foreskin, it must serve some purpose so its removal seems difficult to rationalise. Ohr HaChayim sees a more fundamental difference running through Turnus Rufus' and Rabbi Akiva's conversation, than merely two opinions as to whether we can change God's creation.

Turnus Rufus relates to the act of circumcision in purely physical terms. Rabbi Akiva, however, has a more spiritual perception. God's original intention in creating the world was that humans not be burdened with physical endeavours, such as producing bread from wheat. Everything in the Garden of Eden was 'ready to eat'. Only after Adam and Eve's sin and expulsion from Eden, did the curse of needing 'to earn bread by the sweat of his brow' come into being, thus, the process of milling the flour, kneading the dough and baking the bread is more about remove the stain of impurities resulting from sin, than the physical act of making bread! In this way Rabbi Akiva suggests that the religious obligation of Brit Milah is not just to remove the physical. It removes spiritual impurity *and* introduces an ongoing sacred and holy focus to refine ourselves in all that we do.

The 13th century book *Sefer HaChinuch* emphasises this point, writing: "God wanted the act of circumcision to be performed by the human hand, teaching us that just as we can complete our physical form through Brit Milah, so too can we hone our spiritual selves through noble and creditable actions." He also explains that this sign of our mutual covenant with God is sealed in the flesh of the male reproductive organ so that the perpetuation of Jewish life is associated with the message of Brit Milah, from the earliest possible moment.

The *Talmud*[3] applies the verse[4] "I rejoice with Your instructions like one who has found a large treasure" to the *Mitzvah* of Brit Milah. The Talmud explains that, "Any commandment, like that of circumcision, which the Jewish people accepted with rejoicing is still performed with rejoicing." No matter how adverse the circumstances, or how oppressive the persecutions throughout the ages, this *mitzvah* has continued to be observed faithfully and joyously. Why should this particular mitzvah be performed with so much rejoicing?

The answer lies in perceiving the profundity within this mitzvah. We are created 'incomplete,' *so that* we may rejoice in our capacity to complete – not just physically but also morally, spiritually and religiously – God's ultimate design. Brit Milah is not just a physical act, it is also a sign and reminder of our capacity to act with dignity and responsibility at every moment of our lives. It reminds us of our ability to improve this world, to influence and change things for the better. As this mitzvah represents such grand possibilities, we can understand why it is performed with such rejoicing.

Notes:

1 Leviticus 12:3
2 Midrash Tanchuma
3 *Shabbat* 130a
4 Psalms 119: 162

38 A Soldier's Boots

Lieutenant Colonel Jacob Goldstein

One of the first tasks you learn as a soldier is how to shine your boots. No matter where you're stationed or what your mission, your day begins with polished boots.

When my men and I arrived at Ground Zero, fires were raging out of control and the smoke was burning our eyes. The first thing I noticed was the ash. Cars, people, buildings – everything was covered in ankle-deep ash. Some time later it occurred to us that many people who had been inside the World Trade Cente had been completely burned, cremated by the intense heat of the explosions and fires. This ash was their remains.

I did not clean my boots that night. How could I? Would it make a difference? Within four hours I would be back outside, amid the carnage and destruction. I have not shined my boots since September 11, and when my mission here is completed and I am no longer needed at Ground Zero, these boots will be buried, never to be worn again.

The question I heard every day, from soldiers, civilians, politicians and rescue workers was, "How could God allow this to happen?" They asked me this as I walked on the ashes, as I climbed over destroyed buildings, and as I passed the constant stream of families in mourning, peering over the barricades. I could tell them that there are people who choose to do good and people who choose to do evil. But what do I say to the thousands of innocent people who are suffering, the victims and the bereaved? What can I offer? I can only try to offer hope.

Essentially, my job is hope. I am not trained in desert warfare, I cannot fly an F-16, and I get stuck sometimes just trying to send e-mail. But I do know the value that Judaism places on hope and faith. The *Talmud* teaches us that even if the blade of an enemy's sword is at one's throat, one must never give up hope.

Inside every person there is an incredible reservoir of hope and strength. I have seen it in the Armed Forces for 26 years. But September 11 exposed this hope in each and every person.

I saw hope in a firefighter who stood on burning debris with his boots melting, hoping to find survivors. I saw hope in the eyes of a rescue worker who pulled a kippah out of the wreckage and gave it to me, hoping that I could find out to whom it belonged.

I saw hope in a volunteer who heard that I was going to blow the *shofar* at Ground Zero on *Rosh Hashanah*. When she heard the notes of the shofar, tears began to stream down her face. When the service was over, she gathered herself together, took a deep breath and went back to work.

I saw hope and strength in the Army combat engineers who built a *succah* at Ground Zero for rescue workers and families of the Jewish faith. I heard hope in the words of President Bush and Governor Pataki. I saw hope in the actions of Mayor Giuliani, who was constantly with the workers, encouraging them and thanking them for their help. These ordinary people, these rescue workers, these leaders, help give us hope and faith in a time when we need it most.

A grandfather was talking to his grandson about how he felt. He said, "I feel as if I have two wolves fighting in my heart. One wolf is full of anger, despair and hopelessness. The other is full of compassion, strength and hope."

The grandson asked, "Which wolf will win this fight in your heart?"

The grandfather answered, "The one that I feed."

If there is one thing we need most today, it is hope. Feed the hope and faith in yourself and others around you. Never give up. Never lose hope, as it is the essential ingredient with which we will rebuild our society. Without it, we have buildings that can be destroyed. With it, we are one nation under God, indivisible.

Reprinted with permission from the author.

39 The Art of Giving

Ephraim Mirvis

Many Londoners remember where they were on that Thursday night in January 2003 when an unexpectedly severe snowstorm brought the city to a standstill.

As a result my *Shabbat* sermon that week was devoted to the subject 'Snow and the Jewish People' and I discovered on the internet that the Eskimos use 24 different words for snow. Because it is so crucial to their daily lives, they notice patterns, shapes and nuances which we fail to appreciate. Clearly, the more terms you use for something, the more important it is in your life.

This brings me to the art of giving. In our traditional sources, there are no less than seven different terms used for a present, reflecting the extent to which gifts are central to our Jewish psyche and way of life. Let us have a look at these different terms.

MATANAH: This is the most basic form of present. Coming from the root *natan* – to give, the essence of matanah is the fact that it is given. It is not so much what the gift is but rather that the right thing has been done. So, if one is invited for a meal, one might give a present, but would not enquire beforehand whether the hosts prefer red or white wine, roses or lilies. The main focus is that the deed is correctly done and graciously received.

SHAI: This is an elaborate present – a gift . Here, the giver thinks carefully about the needs and tastes of the receiver and goes to much effort to give something that will be cherished. Shai will be wrapped and properly presented. In similar fashion, in English, there are gift shops but not present shops. We use gift wrap but not present wrap.

BERACHAH: This is a general term for all presents. The word berachah means both to increase and to bless, accurately reflecting the dual role of the giver who is blessed by God for his actions, and of the receiver whose resources are increased.

TERUMAH: This is a contribution to a cause of value, a charity or a needy cause, which one gives in response to an approach that has been made. Terumah comes from the root *ram,* meaning "elevated", indicating that this reactive act of kindness enobles and uplifts the giver.

NEDAVAH: This is an unsolicited contribution to a worthy cause. Being aware of a particular need, one is moved to proactively contribute. The original nedavah is found in the context of "Asher Yidvenu Libo" – every person whose heart makes him willing to give.[1]

DORON: This is a special presentation intended to be treasured and kept for a long time. The root is probably *dor* – generation, indicating that the object will be of longterm value.

MINCHAH: This is the ultimate form of a present. *Onkelos* translates minchah as *tikruvtah,* which means both sacrifice and closeness. From here we see that this *ideal* form of gift must involve an element of sacrifice. The giver gives up something of value to please the receiver, as a result of which bonding takes place.

That the holy Hebrew language, in which every word is precious, contains so many similar yet subtly different words teaches us an essential lesson. As Jews we must appreciate the importance of giving. If we are to emulate our creator, the act of giving in all its forms should be at the heart of our actions and desires. Moreover one can give not only with money, but with time and energy as well and the *Talmud* tells us that wherever selflessness, compassion and kindheartedness are displayed, God's presence is manifested in our midst. In fact the prophet Isaiah records the promise of a greater reward for those who *comfort* the unfortunate than for those who merely give them money.

I will close with a favourite anecdote, which puts the act of giving into perspective. A guest in the home of Amschel Rothschild, the founder of the family dynasty, once turned to his host and enquired, with much *chutzpah*, "How rich are you? I have heard conflicting views on the precise value of your fortune."

Rothschild was not taken aback. He went over to his desk, opened a drawer and took out a folder with the word *Tzedakah* printed on it and proceeded to tot up some figures.

His guest said, "Excuse me. Perhaps you didn't hear what I said. I asked you what you have. I did not ask you what you have given away."

Rothschild smiled and replied, "I heard your question loud and clear. You see, the time will come when, inevitably, I will move on to the next world. Upon my death, I will leave all my material wealth behind. The only thing that I will take with me will be the merit of what I have given." In truth, the only thing that any person really has is that which he has given away!

Notes:
1 Exodus 25:2

40 Shabbat: A Gift Forever

Esther Jungreis

Before his deportation to *Auschwitz*, my grandfather of blessed memory gathered all the sacred vessels of the synagogue and his home and buried them in the courtyard. The Nazis, in their typical methodical manner, had their German shepherds sniff out any objects that may have been hidden there. They found and took everything – everything, that is, but a lone *Shabbat* candelabra, the only item that somehow escaped them. After the liberation, a survivor from my grandfather's congregation returned to the village and found the candelabra. He searched far and wide for a family member and discovered that my father, the only surviving son of my grandfather, was living in New York. And so it was that we received the package containing that precious treasure. The Nazis had robbed us of our home. They had taken all our possessions. They had tortured and killed our loved ones. But there was one thing they could never take away from us – Shabbat. The candelabra that came to us from the ashes was a symbol of that. "My precious little ones, do you know why this candelabra was saved for us?" my father asked. "So that we might teach our brethren to kindle the Shabbat lights."

Another remarkable symbol of the eternal gift of Shabbat came from my father-in-law of blessed memory, Rabbi Yisroel HaLevi Jungreis. He was born on Shabbat and died on the Shabbat before the deportations to the concentration camps, in the year which in Hebrew spells Shabbat. I never had the privilege of meeting him, but I felt I knew him from the many wonderful stories my husband related about his life. He was noted for his *Torah* wisdom, his devotion to the flock and his boundless love of the holy Shabbat. He wrote a scholarly book called *Zachor V'Shamor (You Shall Remember and Observe),* in which he demonstrated that every portion of the Torah is somehow connected to Shabbat. The flames of Auschwitz enveloped my husband's entire family, leaving him and his older brother, Amram, the sole survivors of what was once the great rabbinic house of my father-in-law.

After that horrible conflagration, we had no desire to return to Hungary, yet the grave site of my husband's father was always on our minds. Some 16 years ago, Larry, a member of our congregation, told us that he was going on a business trip to Hungary. "Could you go to Gyongyos (the city where my father-in-law served as a rabbi for over 40 years and where he was brought to his final rest)? Could you visit the cemetery and look for his tombstone?" we asked.

Willingly, Larry undertook the mission, but little did he realise what it would entail. When he arrived in Gyongyos, no one seemed to know the location of the Jewish cemetery. After some inquiries, someone finally directed him there, but it was surrounded by an iron gate, which was locked. Having committed himself to locating that grave site, he wasn't about to give up, so he went to the town hall, where he was told that there was one lone Jew left in Gyongyos and it was he who held the key to the cemetery. When Larry knocked on the old man's door and told him that he had come on behalf of Rabbi Jungreis, the son of the Chief Rabbi of Gyongyos, the old man's eyes filed with tears. "I've been waiting for this day for years – now I can die in peace."

Having said that, he climbed onto a stool, reached up to the top shelf in the kitchen and brought forth a little packet. "This belongs to your Rabbi. I kept it safe all these years, waiting and hoping that someone from the family would appear. You must give it to your Rabbi as soon as you get back to the States," he insisted. The old man took Larry to the cemetery, opened the iron gate and pointed to an overturned tombstone hidden by weeds. "This is the Rabbi's grave." "How can you know that?" Larry asked. "I know. I remember when the Rabbi died and exactly where he was buried. Hoodlums overturned the tombstones and vandalised the cemetery, but I know this is it."

Larry bent to lift the tombstone and through some miracle, he was able to do so. And there, engraved on the stone in Hebrew, was my father-in-law's name and an inscription detailing his life of service to his people and to Torah. A week later, Larry delivered the package from the old man to my husband. It was the only copy of my father-in-law's book, *You Shall Remember and Observe,* written on the subject of Shabbat.

My husband's family home was destroyed. All its contents were looted by the Nazis and the local residents. Nothing remained, but by some miracle, this lone book on Shabbat survived the flames and was waiting to return to its rightful heirs.

The story does not end here. Some years later, I was invited by the Hungarian government to address members of the Jewish community. After I fulfilled my official obligations, I visited the grave sites of my father-in-law and my great-great grandparents, who were all rabbis. I wept, I prayed, I poured my heart out and related to them all that befallen us – the murder of our family in Auschwitz as well as our resurgence in America. I told them that, blessed be God, I had children and grandchildren who carried their names and continue their lives of commitment to Torah.

Upon returning to the States, I received an unexpected phone call. Through yet another miracle, the Shabbat candelabras of my great-grandparents and the Shabbat *Kiddush Cup* of my father-in-law, the Rabbi of Gyongyos, which had been buried during the war, had been found.

Today my father-in-law's book has been read by thousands of Jews across the world. His *Kiddush* cup and the candelabra of my grandfather and great-grandfather grace my Shabbat table. I light each and every one of them and my little grandchildren love to gaze at their scared lights. "*Bubba,*" they plead, "could you tell us the story?" "But I told you the story already. You know it." "Please, Bubba, we want to hear it again."

So I tell them the story of the Shabbat candelabra that triumphed over the flames of Auschwitz, the Shabbat candelabra that is more powerful then any crematoria, the Shabbat candelabra that is a symbol of our eternity.

41 A Taste of Kabbalah

Tziporah Heller

Kabbalah has become a buzzword. For some people it is a sort of religiously oriented white magic, witchcraft with a Jewish bent if you will. For others it is a look inward. Esther (aka Madonna) views it as the ultimate spiritual fix. In fact, it unifies so many elements of Jewish thought as to make diminution of its depth almost inevitable. Therefore, traditionally, it is only studied by foremost scholars. Nonetheless, we will scratch the surface of this complex aspect of Judaism.

'Kabbalah' literally means, "that which was received". This of course raises several questions. From whom? When? By whom? How do we analyse it?

Let us work backwards. Jewish tradition presents the Torah as a multi-layered document. The outside and most easily accessible layer, is called 'pshat', translated as the 'straightforward meaning'. Pshat provides us with structure (through the commandments) and example (through the stories), teaching us how to nurture meaningful connections with God and others, and how to become better people.

The next layer is 'remez', meaning 'hint'. This layer focuses on the choice of wording used in the Torah. It explores textual allusions, number values, and stylistic innovations. The word of God must be studied carefully to grasp the depth of its meanings, as best as we can.

The third layer is 'drush', meaning 'search'. This comprises elusive insights, comparative text reading, and search for deeper meaning in the literal meaning of the words. Only after penetrating these layers, can we attempt the final layer. The fourth layer is called 'sohd', meaning secret. This is an esoteric layer of Torah, which, in sharp distinction to the other layers, cannot be learned by textual analysis. It must be taught by a master and received by a disciple. Thus it is called Kabbalah.

While Kabbalah is as integral to the Torah as the other layers, relegating it to mere intellectual activity misses it's point. The message of Kabbalah is to discover more deeply how God relates to you. If God is unknown to you, it is perhaps because you have excluded Him from your life. If somebody does not want to create a connection to Him, then Kabbalah is not relevant to them.

Like the other layers mentioned above, Kabbalah was received and transmitted by Moses. It was retained as an unwritten tradition, with the exception of a few cryptic manuscripts. The primary classic work of Kabbalah is called Zohar, which was written primarily in the second century CE. It is a running commentary on the Torah and was initially restricted to a small circle, but after centuries of concealment it was eventually published.

Kabbalah entered a new stage with the teachings of a famous 16th century Rabbi, Yitzchak Luria, known by the acronym 'Arizal'. He lived in Sefad in the mid 1500's and was a master of Kabbalah in his era and arguably of any time thereafter. At that time, the suffering experienced by the Jewish people led to hopelessness. The Arizal decided that aspects of the Kabbalah, talking of better times ahead, needed to be publicised. In just two years, his eight volume work, known as Kitvei Arizal, was complied by his chief disciple, Rabbi Chaim Vital.

Briefly stated, these are some of his central ideas:

1 – The significance of different Names of God: Arizal explain that they give us access to God and that each one of the letters of the Names has enormous symbolism. If I saw a friend across the street and shouted "Alice" the implication is that I know exactly who I mean. The exposition of Divine names deepens our perception of Who we mean when we say God.

2 – The doctrines of 'tzimzum' (literally contraction) and the ten 'Sfirot' (attributes): This tells how God moved towards us by contracting his unknowable light and presenting Himself to us via his Names (which are revelations of His being). It also

relates to the way He tells us His story by revealing Himself to us via His involvement in the world. The 10 Sfirot are the guide to understanding this. Additionally, God adapts various roles so to speak, through which His Sfirot can be observed from different angles. This is analogous to observing human traits from various perspectives, such as a parent or a child.

3 - Each commandment provides us with the ability to connect our own spiritual essence to its root from God. Kabbalah reveals the nature of this process.

4 - Our souls have a spark of infinity. That means we are not limited by one lifetime, and Kabbalah explores reincarnation.

5 - Everything comes ultimately from God. Every material object has a spiritual purpose, and every challenge can be overcome and lead us closer to God.

Authentic Kabbalists live with a consciousness of God that is strongly guided by the five steps outlined above.

Nothing could be further from the superstitious magic that passes for Kabbalah in some circles today.

The light of Kabbalah has been filtered down and made accessible to us, while still retaining its authenticity. There are numerous books written by scholars who learned from true masters and became masters on their own. There are many *Chassidic* and other works, which, for those who are ready, can explain the depths of Kabbalah.

No red strings required.

42 Why do Bad Things Happen to Good People?

Shlomo Riskin

This age-old question plagues every religionist, and it is an especially poignant question today in Israel after we have experienced three horrific years of suicide bombings, acts of wanton terrorism which have taken the lives of well over 1,000 innocent and righteous men, women and children.

Our Torah teaches: "When you happen to come upon a nest of birds... chicks or eggs, and the mother is sitting on the chicks or eggs, you must not take the mother along with her young. You must first chase away the mother, and only then may you take the young; then it will be good for you and you will live a long life." [1]

Tragically, there have been many instances during this period of bus-bombings, drive-by shootings and hotel explosions on seder night, in which mothers together with their children were taken to their eternal resting place. It seems as though the Almighty has not fulfilled one of his own *Mitzvot*; something that flies in the face of the principle that God keeps his own Torah.

The Sages of the *Talmud* expand upon this particular command in a way which touches upon – even exacerbates – our question: "If someone as he is praying the *Amidah* before the congregation says 'Your compassion extends even unto a nest of birds', he must be silenced." [2]

The *Talmud* explains: "What is the reason? ... One Sage says, 'it makes the ways of the Divine, matters of compassion, and they are in truth arbitrary decrees'" [3]. Let us attempt to analyse this statement. To what is this Sage referring? He cannot be saying that our Biblical commandments are merely whimsical decrees, because the Torah itself iterates and reiterates that the commands have a purpose; are "*letov lecha* – for your well-being!" In this case, for example, by not taking all of the birds for our own selfish gratification, by holding back from taking the chicks before the concerned eyes of a mother creature, we are training ourselves in the art of self-discipline, and we are demonstrating sensitivity to the parental feelings. We are paving the way for filial respect from generation to generation.

Indeed, this Talmudic Sage is not referring to the commandments but rather to the ways of the Almighty, the "traits of God" which we perceive in this world which seem to be arbitrary decrees based upon the "fate of the draw," the happenstance of genes, the coincidence of circumstance. The Biblical commandment is telling us how to act for our own good; and the addition to prayer, on the basis of a particular interpretation of the commandment is saying that God runs this world on the basis of compassion, which is not true to our human experience.

In fact, the Talmud records an incident in which a father asked his young son to climb a tree and bring him down a pigeon. The child climbed the tree, sent away the mother pigeon, and began to carry down the baby pigeon – thereby fulfilling two commandments (filial devotion and sending away the mother bird) which both promise long life. The child fell from the tree and died.

The Talmud continues and tells us that Rabbi Elisha Ben Abuyah saw this tragic incident, cried out, "there is no Judge and no judgement," and became a heretic. His grandson, Rabbi Yaakov, explained that had the Sage only understood a fundamental axiom of Jewish theology, he would have remained a great teacher in Israel. That axiom is, "there is no reward for the commandments in this world." This world is based upon freedom of choice, the free will of individuals – partners and not puppets – to choose the blessing or the curse, to perfect the world or destroy the world. Were the Almighty to reward the righteous and punish the wicked in this world, everyone who wished long life would live in accordance with the commandments, the Torah would be reduced to a cash machine (You put in filial observance, you take out long life), and our freedom of choice would be severely compromised.

Since we believe in the eternity of the soul; a life after life in another dimension of a world of the spirit, that is the dimension in which Divine reward and punishment takes place. Perhaps the extent to which we develop the light, the good, the spiritual aspect of our personalities and diminish the dark, evil and bestial aspect of our personalities – in this world, will prepare the extent of the spiritual existence we will enjoy in the dimension-to-come. But there is no reward for commandments in this world.

Given this theological perspective, it is then clear why we must silence the *chazzan* who declares that God's compassion in this world extends "even unto a nest of pigeons." We can even dismiss the question "Why do bad things happen to good people?" as being irrelevant in this prior, ante-world in which "children, long life and material sustenance are dependent not on merits but rather on luck (mazal)." [4]

Indeed the only relevant question must be, "what ought good people do when bad things happen to them?" And Toby Weisel, a most beloved resident of Efrat, answers, "They must become even better people." In the words of Rabbi J.B. Soloveitchik, they must turn cruel fate into redemptive destiny. When Rabbi Moshe Ebstein realized that his beautiful babies were born deaf, he initiated the first Hebrew Institute for the Deaf. When the thirteen-year-old Koby Mandel was mutilated to death by a Palestinian terrorist, his mourning parents Rabbi Seth and Sherry organized Camp Koby for survivors of terrorist attacks. Are these super-human responses? Perhaps they are, but the Bible tells us that all who are created in God's image are all part – Divine. Apparently it is only when we realize our super-human potential that this world of tears and travail will be redeemed.

Notes:

1 Deuteronomy 22:6,7
2 Mishnah Berachot 5:3
3 Babylonian Talmud Berakhot 33b
4 Babylonian Talmud Yevamot 28

43 Finding Love in the Maelstrom

Lawrence Kelemen

Twenty years ago, standing on the wet, beautifully tended electric-green grass at the Babi Yar ravine in Ukraine[1], I imagined that I understood Jewish history. I believed it was a story driven by two mechanisms – one natural, the other divine.

The Holocaust and other dark times in Jewish history were purely the natural mechanism, which I dubbed: *"The Law of Evolution of Nations."* This law specified that a nation only survives until its existence is successfully challenged by its neighbours. Ultimately every nation experiences a moment of weakness, and disappears. As evidence that holocausts are normal, I adduced the downfalls of Babylonia, Greece, Rome and other civilisations right through to the Soviet Union. All these nations experienced their respective sunrise and sunset. Accordingly, there was nothing unusual about Jewry being targeted, since eventually all nations meet the same fate.

I also felt I could explain the flipside of the coin: Jewish survival. This, however, required belief in a supernatural mechanism, given the recurring extraordinary circumstances that have allowed the Jews to escape annihilation – such as the sudden death of 185,000 Assyrian soldiers the night before their planned conquest of Jerusalem in 545 BCE, or the mighty Greek army's retreat in the face of a few hundred *Maccabees* in 164 BCE, or the 1948 surrender of the five most powerful mechanised armies in the Middle East to a ragged band of Holocaust survivors, only half of whom actually had guns.

My understanding was that God made a covenant with Jewry and He would ensure that we did not disappear, as long as there were still Jews living by that Covenant. National Jewish survival is thus *quid pro quo*. So that if we climb above our human self-seeking nature, by allowing the Torah to be our guide, we merit – as a nation – to climb above the universe's natural destructive forces and exist above the maelstrom.

The Problem

The idea that holocausts are natural sounds very reasonable when all you have is a Western education behind you and a beautiful, picturesque and scenic ravine in front of you. Neither conveys the unique fury of anti-semitism, the absolute apathy of our neighbours, or the degradation and the terror. The present-day picturesque scene at Babi Yar does not convey what it sounded and looked like sixty years ago when, in only 48 hours, 34,000 Jewish men, women and children were stripped, beaten, driven into the ravine and machine gunned to death. Similarly, history books dull the picture's resolution. There is something sobering about the reality – about staring at the meat hooks on which live Jews were hung at Mathausen, watching Palestinians dancing through the streets of Ramallah waving the entrails of Israeli soldiers, and witnessing the decapitations of Jewish boys like Daniel Pearl – which books cannot illustrate, and which makes their suffering more difficult to understand. Not that only Jews have been tortured and killed. In our generation we have seen many innocent peoples slaughtered, from Sudan to Indonesia and from Chechnya to the Congo. However, frequently these victims were killed because they were in the wrong place at the wrong time. They were not hunted down from country to country, neither were they made into soap or lampshades; and their persecution was never that permanent. Jewish persecution is unique in those regards.

Moreover there is something lopsided about the way the world relates to Jews, something that is absent from most academic discussions of the phenomenon. The world's feelings toward the Jewish State are significant in this regard, since in modern times, Israel *is* "The Jew". The world now views the Jewish State in the way they historically viewed individual Jews, so that caricatures and cartoons in newspapers no longer target Jews but Israel. It is therefore unsurprising that the European Union designated Israel as the "greatest threat to world peace on the planet"! Not North Korea, despite its explicit nuclear threats, not Iran or Syria, who sponsor terror organisations on three continents, nor any other rogue state – Israel!! Meanwhile, the United Nations (UN) has issued more condemnations of the only democracy in the Middle East than of any other nation, and has devoted *60 percent* of its emergency sessions to the purported misdeeds of Israel – including 'crimes' such as targeting notorious terrorists and the construction of a fence *inside their own country*, to keep suicide bombers from murdering innocent Jewish civilians.

Strangely, the General Assembly has never passed a resolution condemning anti-semitism. In 1964, the American delegation tried to include a reference to anti-semitism in the UN's Convention on Racial Discrimination, but failed because of widespread UN protests that anti-semitism was a question not of race but of religion; whereas in 2003, when the UN drafted its *Resolution on Religious Intolerance*, the term anti-semitism was left out because, as the Irish delegate explained with a straight face, "it is more properly considered under the rubric of *race*."

When the French Ambassador to Britain, at a dinner party, recently criticised Israel for its continuing presence in Gaza and the West Bank, calling the Jewish State "a sh—y little country," the Zionist philosopher Hillel Halkin reacted with shock, "Who at London dinner parties makes nasty remarks about Hindus because India has militarily occupied Muslim Kashmir for half a century? What French diplomat calls China a 'big, sh—y country' because of its occupation of Tibet?" Halkin, a man who believed that having our own state would restore the Jews to the family of man, confessed that this failure "is a bitter reality to accept." Having a state has not normalised Jewish existence, it has just become a convenient and visible target for a destructive force that throughout history has defied rational explanation.

The theory I relied upon for so long – that anti-semitism is just a natural phenomenon, another ordinary hatred – rang hollow. At some point I had to accept that in the same way that there is nothing natural about the details of Jewish survival, so too there is nothing natural about Jewish destruction. I needed a new explanation of our tragedies, and I found one in a book written nearly 2,000 years ago.

What I Now Believed

The *Talmud* provides an eyewitness account of Jerusalem just after Rome destroyed the city. *Rabbi Yochanan ben Zakai* is wandering amidst the rubble and sees a starving Jewish woman picking grains of barley out of a dung-heap. This woman, the daughter of one of Jerusalem's wealthiest Jews, tells Rabbi Yochanan that the destruction of Jerusalem has reduced her to scavenging for food, whereupon he remarks: "How fortunate are the Jews! When they do the will of God, no nation rules over them; and when they fail to do so, He places them under the rule of the most degraded nations."

Rabbi Yochanan understood that *both* conditions reflect Jewry's good fortune. Every other nation has been handed over to an intermediary – to nature. As such, there are natural limits as to how high a nation can soar and for how long, and there are natural limits as to how low they can sink. The fortune of every other nation has a floor and a ceiling. Not so for the Jews. Our relationship with the Almighty is too intimate, we are his beloved. When our people cling to God and read his Torah as a love letter, we can find ourselves above the world of Nature. Equally, if Jewry lets go of God, there is no natural safety net; there is no limit to how far we can fall and we can experience horrors that would be impossible within the natural realm. Rabbi Yochanan was able to see our good fortune even in the midst of the maelstrom, because our tragedies and survival both testify to an existence outside of the natural realm.

This article originally appeared in a different version in Jewish Action Magazine, Fall 2004.

Notes:

1 Babi-Yar – on the outskirts of Kiev – is the location of one of the most gruesome acts of mass murder of WWII. However, Jews were forbidden from erecting any memorial there, even decades after the war.

44 A Gutte Yid

Yitzchak Rubin

Yiddish words have infiltrated the English language to such an extent that they've made it into the dictionary. Words such as *chutzpah, mentsch* and *schlepp* can be heard peppered throughout the vernacular. However, there is a lesser known expression, which is even more central to us as a people: "a gutte Yid."

"A gutte Yid" is used to describe a person who is extremely spiritual and close to God. In Eastern Europe, it was used to describe righteous people but fell into disuse after the Holocaust. The expression may have been forgotten by many but the concept has remained strong, for throughout our history the Jewish nation has survived only because such exemplary souls existed.

In late 18th century Russia, a plague broke out in one of the Jewish communities. The Rebbe of Chernobyl could not rest until he found someone who would take him to the neighbouring village so that he could impart some kind of comfort and support.

A secular journalist wrote about what he witnessed, "The reader will well know that I am a proud secularist and that I have little time for these antique remnants, the *chassidim* and their old fashioned ideas. However, last night I saw the Rebbe from Chernobyl and the experience has shocked me to the core. The Rebbe is a short, thin man, with a white beard. He has the saddest yet sweetest eyes I have ever seen and there seems to be a smile on his lips that never ceases as he prays quietly. He came to our stricken town with a mission; he would offer strength and dignity to the many sick and dying and somehow strengthen every one at their own level. Did he succeed? I'm not sure, but one thing I can say, I never thought I would ever say: I believe in human angels! But to have seen this little old man sit with the weary and broken, to have watched as he took their pain and made it his own, to have seen his total connection with every broken heart, is to have witnessed a truly angelic act!"

The "gutte Yid" takes others' pain and makes it his own, and in this way, he allows the stricken to gain comfort. We have seen this in other generations, as well. Imagine the manner in which our *tzaddikim* supported and empowered the horror-stricken Jews that had survived the death camps. The tzaddikim actually reshaped the broken souls by sharing in the pain of their fellow survivors.

I remember seeing the Bobover Rebbe on the eve of *Kol Nidrei* night many years ago. A Jew who had survived the camps had become stricken with a deadly disease and had to have his voice box removed. The sickly Jew came to pray in the Rebbe's synagogue that holy night. And as the Rebbe walked around holding a Torah scroll, chanting the age old *Yom Kippur* prayer, he came upon this weeping soul. The Rebbe embraced him whilst still holding the Torah, creating a trio of *kedushah*: the tzaddik, the sickly Jew and God's Torah. We then witnessed what can only be described as the opening of the floodgates of tears as the Rebbe sobbed together with the voiceless man. The Rebbe was absorbing the man's fears and pain – giving them a voice. This typifies the paradigm of a "gutte Yid."

Where does such strength of spirit come from? One of our most cherished prophets, Elisha, promotes the template of what a "gutte Yid" does. Elisha is always there for others. First, he is there for a destitute widow that others have seemingly turned their backs on. Later, he gives a blessing to an infertile woman and she is soon blessed with child. However, the poor woman faces greater sorrow when that child dies. She runs to the one light that has been constant in her world, the "gutte Yid," the man of God, Elisha. She lays the dead body on Elisha's bed and departs. He brings the child back to life. He revives the dead child, using his own life force for the sake of this youngster.

The prophet is prepared to go beyond the natural forces of this world; he accepts no borders when it comes to helping his fellow man.

Where did Elisha find such incredible spiritual strength? How is it that a tzaddik can override the natural world?

The Torah recounts the life of the first Jew, Abraham, who was also the first "gutte Yid." Abraham provides the blueprint for future Jews to emulate. As the first Jew, he shines forth in the darkness with his overwhelming compassion for others. In Genesis, Abraham is sitting at the doorway of his tent. He has just undergone a traumatic operation, his own circumcision. God visits him. In the middle of his conversation with God, Abraham gets up and runs out to extend hospitality to some dusty nomads.[1] Here Abraham is speaking to God, yet he breaks off his conversation to help some unknown shleppers! This is an awesome display of selflessness.

Our Torah history is replete with loving and giving characters, who would give their own essence away for another soul in need.

Today, we inhabit a world which cannot readily understand such deeds. At a time when success is gauged by one's bank account, or the size of one's home, it is hard to accept that the "gutte Yid" still exists. But Jews do know and should realise how blessed we are that in these dark times we still have such eternal beacons of light.

Notes:
1. Genesis 18:1-3.

45 Mikveh: Gateway to Purity

Rivkah Slonim

A modern-day *mikveh* looks very much like a miniature swimming pool. In a religion rich with detail, beauty and ornamentation – the mikveh is a surprisingly nondescript, humble structure. Its ordinary appearance, however, belies its primary place in Jewish life. The mikveh offers the individual, the community, and the nation of Israel the remarkable gift of purity and holiness. In fact, no other religious establishment, structure, or rite can affect the Jew in this way and on such an essential level. Its extraordinary power, however, is contingent on its construction in accordance with the numerous and complex specifications outlined in *Halacha* – Jewish law.

Immersion in the mikveh has offered a gateway to purity ever since the creation of man. The *Midrash* relates that after being banished from the *Garden of Eden*, *Adam* immersed himself in a river that flowed from the gardens as part of his attempt to return to his original perfection. Before the revelation at *Mount Sinai*, all Jews were commanded to immerse themselves in preparation for coming face to face with God. In Temple times, a Jew who wished to enter the House of God had first to immerse in a mikveh. On *Yom Kippur*, the holiest of all days, the high priest was allowed entrance into the innermost chamber of the Temple, only after five successive immersions in the mikveh.

Put simply, immersion in a mikveh signals a change in status. A woman who from the onset of her menses is in a state *niddut*, separated from her husband, may after immersion be reunited with him in the ultimate holiness of married intimacy. Similarly, those who in Temple times, were precluded from services because of defilement, could, after immersion, enter the House of God. The case of the convert is most striking, as an integral part of conversion to Judaism, the individual who descends into the mikveh as a gentile emerges from beneath its waters as a Jew. Finally, it is the focal point of the purification rite of a Jew before the person is laid to his eternal rest and the soul ascends on high.

The primary uses of mikveh today are delineated in Jewish law and cover diverse elements of Jewish life. But the most important and common usage of mikveh is for purification by the menstruant woman within a framework known as *taharat hamishpachah* – family purity. This observance and subsequent immersion in the mikveh, is a biblical injunction of the highest order. While most Jews see the synagogue as the central institution in Jewish life, Jewish law states that constructing a mikveh takes precedence over building a house of worship. Both a synagogue and a *Sefer Torah*, Judaism's most venerated treasure, may be sold to raise funds for the building a mikveh. It is clearly no exaggeration to state that the mikveh is the touchstone of Jewish life and the portal to a Jewish future.

The concept of mikveh is rooted in the spiritual. Jewish life is marked by the notion of *havdalah*, separation and distinction. On Saturday night, as the Shabbat departs and the new week begins, Jews are reminded of the borders that delineate every aspect of life. Over a cup of wine, we bless God, who "separates between the holy and the mundane, between light and darkness." In fact, the literal definition of the Hebrew word *kodesh*, often translated as "holy," is "that which is separated". In many ways, mikveh is the threshold separating the unholy from the holy. Immersion in a *mikveh* heralds an elevation in status.

In the beginning, the Bible teaches, there was only water. A miraculous compound, it is the primary source and vivifying factor of all substance and, by extension, all life as we know it. But it is more. For these very same attributes – water as source and as sustaining energy – are mirrored in the spiritual. Water has the power to purify, to restore and replenish life to our essential, spiritual selves. The mikveh personifies both the womb and the grave, the portals to life and the afterlife. In both, the person is stripped of all power and prowess. In both, there is a mode of total reliance, complete abdication of control.

Immersion in the mikveh can be understood as a symbolic act of self-abnegation, the conscious suspension of the self. In so doing, the person immersing signals a desire to achieve oneness with the Source of all life, God. It is thus described not only in terms of purification, but also – and perhaps primarily – as rebirth.

Judaism teaches that the source of all *taharah*, purity, is life itself. Conversely, death is the harbinger of *tumah* – impurity. All types of ritual impurity, (and the Torah describes many), are rooted in the absence of life or some measure – even a whisper – of death.

When stripped to its essence, a women's menses signals the death of potential life. Each month a woman's body prepares for the possibility of conception. The presence of potential life within, fills a woman's body with holiness and purity, readying her to serve as a cradle for life. With the departure of this potential, impurity sets in, conferring upon the woman a state of impurity or more specifically, niddut. Impurity is neither evil nor dangerous, and it is not something tangible. Impurity is a spiritual state of being. Only immersion in the mikveh, has the power to change the status of the woman.

The concept of purity and impurity as mandated by the Torah and applied within Jewish life is unique; it has no parallel or equivalent in this postmodern age. Perhaps that is why it is difficult for the contemporary mind to relate to the notion and view it as relevant. In ancient times, however, tumah and taharah were central determining factors.

Most notably, tumah made entrance into the Holy Temple impossible. There were numerous types of impurities that affected Jews. Mikveh immersion was the culmination of the purification rite in every case. As such, the institution of mikveh took centre stage in Jewish life.

While we cannot presently serve God in a physical Temple in Jerusalem, we *can* erect a sacred shrine within our lives; there remains one arena in which purity and impurity continue to be pivotal. In this connection only is there a biblical mandate – and that is regarding human sexuality. Lovemaking signals the possibility and potential for new life, the formation of a new body and the descent from Heaven of a new soul. In their fusing, man and woman become part of something larger; in their transcendence of the self, they draw on, and even touch, the Divine. They enter into a partnership with God; they come closest to taking on the Godly attribute of Creator. In fact, the sacredness of the intimate union remains unmitigated even when the possibility of conception does not exist. In the metaphysical sense, the act and its potential remain linked.

Human sexuality is a primary force in the lives of a married couple. A strong relationship between husband and wife is not only the backbone of their own family unit but is integral to the world at large. The blessing of trust, stability, continuity, all flow from the commitment they have to each other. In their private, personal togetherness, they are creators of peace, harmony, and healing—on a microcosmic scale but with macrocosmic reverberations—and as such are engaged in the most sacred of pursuits.

In this light it becomes clear why marital relations are often referred to as the Holy Temple of human endeavour. And entrance to the Holy always was, and continues to be, contingent on ritual purity.

The mikveh cycle and the laws of family purity are a Divine ordinance and it is this that underlies the mitzvah's potency. The knowledge that it is sourced in something larger than the self – that it is not based on the emotions or a subjective decision – allows tarahat hamishpachah to work. Ironically, this "unfathomable" mitzvah reveals its blessings to us more than almost any other in daily, palpable ways.

At first glance, the mikveh system speaks of limitations and constraints – a loss of freedom. In truth, emancipation is born of restriction. Secure, confident, well-adjusted children (and adults) are disciplined children; they understand restraint and ultimately learn self-control. And in no area of life is this more necessary than in our most intimate relationships. There is strength and comfort in the knowledge that human beings cannot fulfil their every whim.

Over time, open-ended sexual availability often leads to a waning of excitement and even interest. Mikveh's monthly hiatus teaches couples to treasure the time they have together. They count the days until they can be together, and each time there is a new quality to their reunion. In this regard, the Talmud states, "So that she will be as beloved as on the day of her marriage."

Furthermore, human beings share a nearly universal tendency for the forbidden. How many otherwise intelligent individuals have jeopardized their marriages and families in pursuit of the illicit because of its seeming promise of the romantic and the new? Mikveh introduces a novel scenario: one's spouse – one's partner in life, day after day, for better and for worse – becomes temporarily inaccessible, forbidden, off limits.

For many women, their time as a niddah also offers them a measure of solitude and introspection. There is, additionally, an empowering feeling of autonomy over their bodies and, indeed, over the sexual relationship they share with their spouses. Most importantly, it encourages the development of a relationship on a spiritual and emotional level and nurtures verbal communication, which in turn further fuels their physical relationship.

The benefits brought to married life by the practice of family purity have been recognized by numerous experts, Jew and gentile alike. Ultimately, however, mikveh's powerful hold on the Jewish people – its promise of hope and redemption – is rooted in the Torah and flows from a belief in God and his perfect wisdom. Judaism calls for the consecration of human sexuality. It is not enough that intimacy be born of commitment and sworn to exclusivity; it must be sacred. By immersing in the mikveh, each woman can link herself to an ongoing tradition that has spanned the generations. Through mikveh she brings herself in immediate contact with the Source of life, purity, and holiness – with the God who surrounds her and is within her always.

46 Coping With Bereavement

Herschel Billet and Harvey Belovski

The concept: Herschel Billet

There is a *Talmudic* aphorism: "*tzarot rabim chatzi nechamah*," "the agonies of the multitude are half a consolation." At first glance this is perplexing. How can one draw comfort from someone else's pain? Their pain brings me neither joy nor eases my pain.

It seems to me, that in reality the Rabbis were making a brilliant observation. In life we know or meet many people who have suffered a loss, a terrible illness, or a debilitating injury. And yet they live a full, productive and even happy life. How do they do it?

Simply, they chose life. They realised that the clock cannot be moved back. Time moves forward. We have but two choices. Either live a quality life, which impacts positively on family, friends, and society, or fall apart which helps no one. In fact, it hurts those whose lives are dependant on ours.

Those that rise beyond their suffering are people who have the right perspective and have asked the correct questions. Undoubtedly, they too have struggled and suffered, however, in the end they made the right choice. What the Rabbis were saying was: "look at the many who suffered and coped. Take half a comfort from them. If they can do it, you too, can do it." The other half of the 'consolation' is up to the individual.

People who have suffered have to draw on a previously unknown inner strength that they discover they have. They also have to allow others to help them. When we make a *shivah* visit, before we leave we say to the mourners, that, "they should find comfort among all other mourners of Zion and Jerusalem." Rabbi JB Soloveitchik once asked, "who are the other mourners of Zion and Jerusalem?" They are the Jewish people of all times, past and present. What we say to the mourner is that you are not the first to suffer a loss. But look how others have found comfort and coped. You too, can and must, draw your strength from those others.

I have found that both personally and for others, these observations have been helpful as coping strategies. May God grant that good people know no further pain and suffering and that He remove tears from the faces of his people.

The Practice: Harvey Belovski

Death is one of the few experiences common to all peoples and each civilization has devised its own ways of dealing with the despair that follows in its wake.

Judaism offers an astonishing, holistic approach to dealing with the anguish of bereavement; one that shows the profound awareness of the human spirit which is inherent in all of Torah life. But sadly, as with many magnificent areas of Jewish tradition, its mourning practices and their raison d'être are scarcely understood.

In truth, shivah is a remarkable strategy for handling the emotional and practical consequences of a death in the family. Anyone struggling with the shock of bereavement yearns to be cocooned for a while from the new realities of life. Mourners also need to acquire the means for coping with the emotional roller coaster set in motion by the loss of a family member. There is also the need to deal with the inevitable guilt associated with separation. During this period, mourners strive to develop a rich mental image by which to remember their departed loved one. Jewish mourning provides all of these needs and more.

During a shiva, the bereaved family members honour the dead by dedicating an entire week to thinking and talking about the deceased; they neglect their regular personal and business activities. Instead they remain at home to concentrate entirely on the qualities and character of their loved one. They withdraw, as it were, from normal worldly engagement by sitting on low chairs, eating food prepared by others and not leaving the shiva-house. They wear the clothes they tore at their moment of grief, thereby keeping their loss uppermost in their minds throughout the week.

The mourners spend their time recounting tales of their departed relative; laughing and crying together as they recall significant events in their shared lives. They might experience periods of anguish, unable to do more than sit bereft, overwhelmed with melancholy. They will be touched by letters and phone calls from far away friends and listen intently to visitors who may recount previously untold stories about the deceased, offering new insight from the perspective of a childhood friend or work colleague. By the end of the shiva, the mourners will have crystallised a mature image of the deceased in their minds, which will accompany them for the rest of their lives.

Beyond this, the cathartic value of shiva is quite incredible. While grief and guilt are at their strongest, the shivah insulates the mourners from having to handle the bleak practicalities of day-to-day life, allowing them to emerge gradually into normality only when the immediate harshness of their loss has passed.

However, helping the mourners to avail themselves of this vital experience, takes great understanding from the visitors to the shiva-house. Jewish law, which excels at understanding our most profound emotional needs, regulates this to perfection. Few of us are aware that one should not even talk to the mourners until they indicate that this is their wish. Perhaps they do not wish to speak. How can we, mere onlookers to a family tragedy, impose on the bereaved in the slightest way? We must be exquisitely sensitive, yet appropriately responsive to the mourners' emotional trauma. If they initiate a conversation, we will respond; should they laugh, we will share the humorous reminiscence; when they cry, we will provide comfort. And should they remain mute, unable or unwilling to speak, we too, will sit in silence. This is how we, as Jews, contribute to the healing process of the bereaved.

Yet unfortunately for many, this means of coping with bereavement will seem unfamiliar, for it is a far cry from the cursory nod to the mourners, pleasant chatter and eating of refreshments that frequently characterise modern shivahs. Our unwillingness to face the reality of our own transience tempts us to downplay the impact of grief on others. As a result, we may treat a shiva as an opportunity to avoid addressing the only certainty of our lives — death itself. Of course, this response to the suffering of others is the precise opposite of the true intention of shivah and it contributes to the mourners' feelings of wretchedness.

In conclusion, these very brief guidelines may help illuminate the concept of shiva, should, God forbid, it become relevant. If you are the bereaved, remember that visitors are there exclusively for your benefit. Have no qualms about resting when you feel tired, asking people to be considerate and gently requesting them to leave when you no longer want to speak. If you are visiting, bear in mind that you are present solely to respond to the needs of the mourners. If possible, visit at a quiet time. Do nothing whatsoever that imposes on the mourners. Empower them to express themselves in their own ways. Leave when the time is right.

I pray that God will bless all of us with long and happy lives, filled with sensitivity to each other and that we will never know the pain of bereavement.

47 Who Will Win This War?

Yaffa Eliach

When Kalman and his sixteen year old son Yitzchak were caught on a Budapest street in the summer of 1944 and placed in a labour battalion, they knew what to expect.

"You are now under the direct command of the Todt Organisation and as such, you are the soldiers of the Third Reich. You are fortunate people who will benefit from the generosity of the German Fatherland." The men listened intently to the German officer's speech and a glimmer of hope appeared on their taut faces. Kalman Mann tried to conceal his bitter smile. He had heard that speech before. The clean-shaven, well-fed, meticulously dressed German officer could no longer fool him. Kalman knew well from firsthand experience what it meant for a Jew in wartime to be a so-called soldier in the Jewish labour battalions. It meant digging anti-tank ditches, building roads and burying murdered Jews.

Life in the labour battalion was even more difficult than Kalman had anticipated. The Germans were now retreating in haste. Food rationing was more meagre than ever, injuries from work were on the increase and because of minimal medical attention, oozing open wounds were everywhere in sight.

On the eve of *Rosh Hashanah*, 1944, the Russians launched a big offensive and the German retreat hastened. The labour battalion was given orders to demolish all communications, transportation and dwellings. Telegraph and electricity poles were sawn into small cubes of lumber, railroad tracks were uprooted, bridges blown up, main highways destroyed and houses set to the torch. Only the scorched earth remained behind the retreating German Army. The labour battalion was constantly on the move, never sleeping in the same location. They were given only a few hours to sleep under the open sky before being moved to the next demolition assignment. On the eve of *Yom Kippur* they reached the Polish mountain of Bornemissza, between Osmoloda and Tacev, on the Slovakian border.

The German commander stepped out from his covered wagon and gave one of the long speeches they had learned to accept as part of their daily suffering. "I know that tomorrow is one of the most important holidays, Yom Kippur. It is an important fast day in your religion. I want to remind you that you are soldiers, soldiers at a time of war on the battlefields, and as such, it is strictly forbidden for you to fast. All those who fast will be executed by a firing squad." They expected him to go on and continue to enumerate the benevolence and righteousness of the German army. But he stopped short and repeated his closing remark: "Violators will be executed by a firing squad."

On Yom Kippur, September 27, they worked as usual. It was an especially difficult day for it rained heavily and everything around them was turning into a muddy swamp. When food was distributed, all the men, as if by prior agreement, spilled the coffee into the running muddy gullies and tucked the stale bread into their soaked jackets.

Kalman Mann and another Jew recited the Yom Kippur prayers, whatever they remembered by heart. All the others repeated after them while their tears mingled with the rain and their voices fought the noises of hammers, axes and the constant downpour of the rain.

And so while demolishing telegraph and telephone poles in the heavy downpour, the men calculated the time to say the closing prayer of this holiest of days, the *Neilah* prayer.

Night came and they fell exhausted at the foot of Mount Bornemissza, ready to break their fast. Just then the German commander and a group of soldiers emerged from their covered wagons and ordered them to line up for roll call. The Jews expected the worst. Fathers parted from their sons, brothers said goodbye to brothers and friends feared for their last moments together.

"I am a benevolent officer in the best German tradition." Their fears intensified for they knew what to expect when they heard one of those "generosity" speeches. It was usually followed by the most catastrophic aftermath. "I know that you fasted today, but I am not going to invoke the death penalty that you deserve according to law. Instead you are going to climb that mountain and slide down on your stomachs. Those among you who would like to repent may say that they were wrong in disobeying army regulations and fasting today. Those who would like to do so please raise your hands." Not a single hand went up.

And so, tired, soaked and starved, the emaciated Jews climbed the wet slippery mountain. When they reached the top they were ordered to slide down on their stomachs. When they reached the bottom, they were ordered to line up again. They were asked if there were individuals who wanted to repent and be spared the ordeal. Mud-covered figures with feverish eyes looked at the clean-shaven officer in silent defiance. And so ten times they repeated the humiliating performance, each time with more determination, each time with more strength, climbing and sliding from an unknown Polish mountain which on that soggy Yom Kippur night became a symbol of Jewish courage and human dignity.

At midnight, as the rain abated, the performance was stopped. The men were given food and drink. They lit small campfires, trying to dry their clothes and warm their shivering bodies. Their faces shone with a strange glow as they sat around the small campfires at the foot of Bornemissza. It seemed as if the campfires reflected the glow of their shining faces and burning eyes.

A young German officer of low rank walked over to the group where Kalman and his son Yitzhak were sitting and said, "I don't know who will win this war, but one thing I am sure of – people like you, a nation like yours, you will never be defeated, never!"

Based on an interview with Rabbi Yitzhak Mann, June 12, 1979

48 The Holocaust: Were They Sheep to the Slaughter?

Aubrey Hersh

As an occasional tour guide to Eastern Europe, and as someone whose parents lived through and survived the war years – though most of my uncles and aunts did not – this is a question that I have confronted both professionally and personally.

In 1971, Yad Vashem organised a conference on 'Jewish resistance in the Holocaust', and acknowledged that while there *were* revolts in various ghettoes (Warsaw, Vilna) and death camps (Sobibor, Treblinka, Auschwitz), physical resistance was limited. The conference addressed the issue of why that was so.

Firstly there was the fact that most Jews – as late as 1944 – were largely unaware of, and unable to believe in, the plans for their mass extinction. As Elie Wiesel writes:

"Hitler was determined to strike at the last Jewish survivors of his empire. Washington knew it, and so did London. But we, in our little town [in Hungary] did not."[1]

The Germans mounted the greatest deception of all time, to allay the fears of the Jews until the very last moment, talking of ressetlement, and (even in their *own* communiqués) of the Final Solution but never of mass murder, gas chambers or death camps. At some camps people were given soap and a towel as they entered the gas chamber; at Maidanek, children were given candy.[2] The deception was so successful that some people *voluntarily* joined the transports to be with their families.[3]

Secondly, the purpose of Jewish resistance during the war generally, although unquestionably noble, was not to live, but to die with honour. This is true of all the major uprisings staged by the Jews (especially Warsaw). A case in point is the famous revolt in Treblinka of August 1943. Of the 700 inmates, hardly 150-200 succeeded in escaping; the rest were killed during the fighting, and only 12 of those who escaped remained alive. The others were caught by the Germans.[4]

Therefore as long as the situation was not hopeless, most Jews did not fight.

Additionally, armed resistance often created morally complex situations.

"In the Vilna Ghetto, the Gestapo Chief, Neugebauer, issued an order declaring that for every Jew who escaped to join the partisans, his family would be taken; if the family was not at hand, those who shared his room would be responsible; if the room tenants could not be found, everybody living in that courtyard would be shot. All the Jews going out to work were to be divided into groups of ten persons. If a group returned from work with anyone missing, the rest of his group would be shot; knowing quite well therefore that in this way they were putting in danger the existence of the whole ghetto and most of all the lives of their dear ones. They would be responsible for the spilt blood."[5]

Furthermore, many people, having lost their *entire* families, could not bring themselves to rise up and endure more pain, suffering and torture, given that it would end in their death anyway. In judging them, we need to ask ourselves, how much was it right to expect from ordinary men, women and children – similar to you or me – who were suddenly and brutally removed from their everyday existence and plunged into a world with no rules, where all that was familiar disappeared, and where values ceased to exist?

Finally and most importantly though, we have to define what we mean by resistance.

Who are actually the heroes in Judaism? Is it only those who carry weapons? What of the parent who deliberately remained behind to look after their children, when they could have escaped? Or the rabbi who stood at head of his flock and accompanied them to their final destination? What of those such as Dr Emmanuel Ringelblum, who wrote diaries and hid them; who risked their lives, to chronicle the fate of the doomed for posterity? Are they then cowards?

What about those who endangered their health for others?

Lena Donat, a pharmacist in the Auschwitz hospital, exchanged beds with her friend Judith when the latter contracted typhus. By hiding her in this manner, Lena saved Judith from the selection. Sleeping in her friend's lice-infested bed, Lena knew that she would become ill within the disease's two-week incubation period. During Lena's subsequent bout with typhus, friends protected her. In this case, as in others, mutual assistance did not ensure survival for all. While Lena recovered, her childhood friend and fellow worker, Ola, caught the disease and died."[6]

Overall, Dr Marc Dworzecki, recognises at least 12 real forms of resistance including. The preserving of human identity, giving up chances to be saved, dying 'Al Kiddush Hashem', sacrifice for the good of the many, moral and religious steadfastness in day-to-day life, cultural resistance, publicising the atrocities, escapes and physical resistance itself. [7]

In fact perhaps the best description of heroism by the Jewish masses, to the Nazi horror, was captured by Shaul Esh:

"It was fundamentally what might be called kiddush ha-hayyim, the sanctification of life. This expression is taken from the late Rabbi Isaac Nissenbaum, one of the Religious Zionist leaders in the Warsaw Ghetto: 'This is a time for kiddush ha-hayyim, the sanctification of life, and not for kiddush Hashem, the holiness of martyrdom. Previously the Jew's enemy sought his soul and the Jew sacrificed his body in martyrdom [i.e. he made a point of preserving what the enemy wished to take from him]; now the oppressor demands the Jew's body and the Jew is obliged therefore to defend it, to preserve his life.' That kiddush ha-hayyim was the general feeling is borne out by all the evidence. It explains the enormous will to live that was emphasized at all times and in all places, in the midst of the basest degradation, a will best expressed by the Yiddish word that was on the lips of the majority of the survivors of the Holocaust – "iberleybn", to survive, to remain alive. The Jews of Eastern Europe felt in fact that victory over the enemy lay in their continued existence, or in providing for the continued existence of others, for the enemy desired their extinction.[8]

Even in cases of physical resistance, the heroism often lay, not only in the deed itself, but in what followed:

When Rosa Robota was able to make contact with some of the slave laborers, she and a group of girls working with her at the Krupp munitions plant at Auschwitz arranged to smuggle out dynamite to the resistance organization in the camp. Some of the girls were caught and hanged. But the smuggling went on. Then, on October 7, 1944, everyone at Auschwitz heard and saw something unbelievable. One of the crematoria, in which the bodies of so many of their mothers, fathers, and young had been burned, was blown to pieces. In an investigation that led to the arrest of Rosa, the SS used all their sadistic methods of torture on her. She betrayed no one. Her last words scribbled on a piece of paper just before she was hanged in front of the assembled inmates at Auschwitz were "Hazak V'Amatz"—Be Strong and Brave."[9]

There were also tremendous acts of spiritual resistance, even under the most trying of circumstances. Viewing the conflict in eschatological terms, as a battle between good and evil, some Jews were able to stay focused on the ultimate aim in life; indeed to view life as having profound purpose even in the hell of a concentration camp. This often took great fortitude:

During Passover of 1945, in a German work camp, Rabbi Samson Stockhamer incredibly refused to eat bread for the eight-day festival with the intention that at least one Jew of the 2,500 interned there should properly observe the dictates of the holiday.[10]

Would anyone refer to any of these individuals as sheep? Would any of us be capable of exhibiting such courage?

Before pronouncing judgement therefore, we have to be aware of the world within which this tortured people existed and of the limited choices that were available to them. It must be understood, that in 1939 it was still inconceivable that man could be so inhuman. Back then, they were still able to believe that there were depths to which a human being would not, indeed *could not* descend. Unfortunately the 20th century has cured us of those illusions.

As one of the survivors explained:

"...the great majority followed the path that appeared most reasonable and that seemed to offer the best chance according to

historical and personal experience. A machine of total extermination was outside of all human experience. There are, of course, other reasons and these are only now becoming better known: the Nazi skill at camouflage and deception; the tremendous military power before which even great nations skilled in war crumbled; and the apathy of neighbours, close at hand or far away."[11]

So that in response to the question, the answer would be: Yes, the Jews in the Holocaust *were* sheep... not to the slaughter, but to the altar, on which they joined 100,000's of Jews throughout our history, who were killed for one crime only – that of being born a Jew. After 60 years it is time to set the record straight and recognise the 6 million dead for what they were – martyrs.

I will close with a not un-typical Holocaust story, of a family from a small town in Slovakia, near Kosice. The husband Heinrich (Chaim) owned a lumber mill on the outskirts of the city. In 1941 he endangered his life by agreeing to become one of the stop-off points for Jewish teenagers being smuggled out of Poland, hiding the frightened children in the crawl space under the timber. Unfortunately in 1942, he was betrayed by one of his non-Jewish workers and killed. His wife fled, leaving everything behind, and found temporary refuge in Hungary, only returning to her hometown in 1943. A few months later however, she retraced her journey to Hungary, leaving a letter with a gentile friend, with instructions that if she didn't come back after the war, the letter should be posted to those of her children that had emigrated to America.

Sadly, she was never heard from again and the letter was duly sent. It reached America and told of her decision to leave the relative safety of her hometown, because another of her children had just given birth to a child in Hungary, and needed her help. She felt it was her duty to be with her daughter, despite the dangers of the journey. This letter was the last the family ever had from their mother.

Having read this account, the question is how would you describe this couple? After all they were both killed and they killed no Germans in return. My own assessment is probably biased; but then it would be, considering that it requires me to judge the actions of my own paternal grandparents[12]. But you who are unbiased, you can be the judge. What would you say? Were they sheep who went to the slaughter, or were they and the other 6 million victims, real Jewish heroes? You tell me.

Notes:
1 Elie Wiesel: Tout les fleuves vont a la mer (1994)
2 Attorney General's Opening Address, Eichmann trial (Chapter IX p. 2)
3 Olga Lengyel, Five Chimneys: The Story of Auschwitz p.4.
4 Yitzchak Arad: Jewish armed resistance in Eastern Europe. (IDF Officers publication –1972)
5 Isiah Trunk: Conference on manifestation of Jewish resistance (Yad Vashem –1971) pp202-277
6 Alexander Donat, Holocaust Kingdom, p. 308
7 Marc Dworzecki: The day to day stand of the Jews (pp152-181)
8 Shaul Esh: The dignity of the destroyed (AJC –1962) pp99-111
9 They Fought Back: The Story of Jewish Resistance in Nazi Europe (New York -1967), pp. 219-225.
10 Eliav, Ani Ma'am Vol I (pp. 220-221)
11 The catastrophe of European Jewry (Yad Vashem 1976)
12 Chaim & Baila Hershkowitz *hy"d*

49 Why Marry Jewish?

Doron Kornbluth

A new executive gets transferred into the headquarters of a major company. He is a good-looking Afro-Carribean guy. One of his fellow employees – a beautiful blonde woman – is very attracted to him. She sits down next to him at the cafeteria. She 'happens' to be there every time he goes for a coffee. He gets the message, and quietly mentions to a mutual friend, "I'm flattered, but to be honest, I only date black women."

Word gets out and the office is in an uproar: some say that he is being racist. He responds that he wants to date someone who can fully share his culture.

Who is right?

The truth is that the way we use the term 'racism' today refers to discrimination against people. He won't give me a job because he thinks that I am inferior to him. That is racism, and it is wrong.

The Afro-Carribean guy above wasn't saying anything against anybody. He would have said the same had she been Indian, Jewish or Argentinean. He was simply doing what he thought was best for his marriage, kids, and heritage. The point is that encouraging same-faith marriage is not racist. It is not *against* anybody. It is *for* us.

But I'm not religious...

Most people agree that a committed church-going Christian and a committed shul-going Jew should not marry. They are just asking for trouble. The chances of success are small, and the kids are at risk. Yet people feel that 'we're not so religious, so it doesn't matter.' However, people's attitudes towards religion and culture change as people marry and settle down. A recent poll[1] found that the least religious time in a person's life was their twenties — meaning that people get re-involved in their heritages later. So even if you don't feel very 'religious' now, the chances are high that one or both of you will change soon. With this in mind, here are a few points to think about:

When musician Billy Joel and supermodel Christie Brinkley were divorced, he said that the main problem they had was geographic. He loved New York and couldn't live anywhere else. She was a California girl who hated New York. They simply couldn't find a place to live where both were happy. When they went back and forth between Los Angeles and New York, one was unhappy at any given time. If they had tried somewhere in the middle, both would be unhappy. This one issue destroyed their marriage.

While we shouldn't be naive enough to think that this was the only reason for their divorce (the real reasons are none of our business), this geographic vignette is an excellent illustration of the importance of practical (non-emotional) factors in marriage. Often, love simply cannot beat practicality, and inter-marriages are much more problematic than same-faith marriages.

As one woman put it, "Nothing is simple. Where to live, what holidays to celebrate, what food to serve, where to send the kids to religious school — everything is a question. Everything ends in an argument. Things that should bring you closer drive you further apart."

Not surprisingly inter-faith marriages, whether involving a Muslim marrying a Hindu, a Catholic marrying a Protestant, or a Jew marrying a non-Jew — report far less happiness and far more divorce than comparable same-faith marriages. [2]

Also kids who grow up in mixed-marriages have a hard time 'fitting in' and finding themselves — they typically report low self-confidence and sense of belonging. No surprise that intermarriage therapists and literature from around the world cite this as the number one problem of intermarriages: the high risk of hurting the kids.[2]

The Jewish Thing...
You may know of individual cases where children of intermarriage stayed Jewish despite one of their parents being

non-Jewish (we're not discussing converts here). Unfortunately, the reality is almost always otherwise. In country after country, in study after study over the last thirty years, it has become abundantly clear that the chances of Jewishness staying alive in inter-married families are very, very low.

To quote just a few facts about the children of inter-marriage:

At most 18% of the children of inter-marriage are being raised as "Jewish only."[3]

Even the minority who are officially being raised as 'Jews only' celebrate Christmas more than they celebrate Passover! [4]

93% give and/or receive Christmas presents [5]

Even when things start out well, "most inter-faith families – even those raising their children as Jews – incorporate substantial Christian celebrations into their lives, often including more Christian aspects as the couple and their children age." [6]

Compared to families with two Jewish parents, mixed-married families are far less likely to be involved in Jewish life, to attend synagogue, to give their children a Jewish education, or to create a Jewish ambience in their home. The intermarriage rate among children of intermarriage exceeds 90 percent. The Jewishness of their families is almost always lost. [7]

Dating

Even if you aren't ready to get married, inter-dating leads to inter-marriage. It's as simple as that. We just never know where feelings will take us and how long a relationship will last. Our emotions get deeper with time, and it gets harder and harder to break it off.

The very fact that you date non-Jews sets a pattern and changes your outlook. If you spend five years romantically involved with non-Jews, get used to Christmas and Easter parties, and to downplaying your Jewishness in order to make your partner feel comfortable, chances are high that your marry-Jewish conviction will drop significantly.

Getting Practical

The good news is that there are millions of single Jews out there of all types, who also would like to find their Jewish soul-mate. How can you meet them? The best way is to get involved. Find a shul with people your age. Participate in classes. Volunteer in Jewish organisations. Join trips to Israel. The more active you are, the more Jews you will meet, and the more possibilities you have to meet 'that special someone.'

Notes:

1 Gallup Poll released to the press on July 14, 1999.

2 see 'Why Marry Jewish? Surprising Reasons for Jews to Marry Jews' by Doron Kornbluth, Targum/Feldheim, 2003

3 Of the rest, 33% are being raised Christian only, 24% in 'No Religion' homes and 25% in 'Dual Religion' homes. 'Re-examining Intermarriage: Trends, Textures, Strategies,' by Dr. Bruce A. Phillips, published by the American Jewish Committee and the Wilstein Institute, 1997, Figure 2-3, p. 49.

4 ibid, Table 2-5, p. 52

5 Egon Mayer, "Children of Inter-marriage: A Study in Patterns of Identification and Family Life", AJC, 1983. 83% of the children of intermarriage perceived "no greater responsibility to fellow Jews than [to] others in need." 70% felt they had no greater responsibility to support Israel than other citizens, or at all. 81% deemed "unimportant" the act of belonging to the Jewish community. Only 9% felt studying about Judaism was very important.

6 "Jewish and Something Else: A Study of Mixed-Marriage Families," by Brandeis Univeristy's Dr. Sylvia Barack-Fishman. Released internationally and given wide publicity in early May, 2001.

7 'Questions Jewish Parents Ask About Intermarriage,' AJC, 1992 Mark Winer and Ayeh Meir, p. 19

50 The Role of Jewish Women Throughout the Ages

Sarah Robinson

The *Torah* writes, "Remember the days of old, understand the years of the previous generations."[1] God encourages us to look into our past because he wants us to learn from it. Therefore, the lives of our matriarchs were recorded in great detail, giving us an opportunity to share in their human experience, their moments of despair and joy, their familial struggles and triumphs as well as their prayers for the future. We are obliged to see these women, who trail-blazed the path of the Jewish nation, as real people who wrestled with many of the same frustrations and aspirations that we face today.

Amongst the myriad stories the Torah recounts about the matriarchs, we read of their devout prayers in pleading for children. And from Hannah we learn the power of prayer such that her demand of God for a child is the *Talmudic* source for the form and content of the *Amidah* prayer. Other biblical women, including Deborah, Yael and Judith, devoted themselves entirely to the cause of the Jewish people with courage and determination, often jeopardising their own personal safety. And Miriam generated optimism and hope for all the Jews as they crossed the Red Sea. She rallied the women so that due and open appreciation could be expressed to God, for their deliverance from the Egyptians.

The *midrash* discusses the Jewish women's pivotal role in the formation of the Jewish nation as the new nation crossed the desert on their way to Israel. In the desert, the Jewish people despaired in their circumstances but it was the women who provided vision and hope, leading by example. As the Midrash states, "In those days the women guarded what the men violated."[2]

Whilst the men danced around the *Golden Calf*, cried out to return to Egypt and believed the ten spies dismal report about Israel, the women maintained their optimism and unwavering faith and refusal to believe the spies' negative report. Therefore, these women were exempt from God's decree that the generation would never set foot in Israel. [3]

They refused to give their jewellery for idol worship, exclaiming, "Why should we sacrifice to a calf that has no power to save?"[4] The women's refusal to give their jewellery for worship of the Golden Calf, saving their donations for the *mishkan*, merited that God would designate *Rosh Chodesh* as a festival in honour of their steadfastness and devotion.

Throughout forty years of struggle in inhospitable environments, internal strife and uncertainty, the women of that generation maintained the optimism and faith necessary for survival of the Jewish spirit. They placed their confidence in God and were determined to follow the path God had outlined for them as the Jewish nation.

It is the manner in which each of these women dealt with the conflicts in their daily lives which educates us today, their struggles imparting an emboldening message, giving us the clarity to identify and fulfil our purpose in the world.

We can see the tradition of independent thought combined with great courage and concern for the future of our people in the words of a more contemporary heroine, Hannah Senesh.

She was prepared to parachute into her native Hungary in an attempt to rescue fellow Jews still under Nazi occupation. She was caught and murdered, leaving the legacy of her diary and poems. At age sixteen, Hannah, encountering prejudice, wrote,

"Only now am I beginning to see what it really means to be a Jew in a Christian society. But I don't mind at all. It is because we have to struggle, because it is more difficult for us to reach our goal, that we develop outstanding qualities." [5]

A year later, before the outbreak of the war, she wrote,

"I don't know whether I've already mentioned that I've become a

Zionist. The word stands for a tremendous number of things. To me it means, in short, that I consciously and strongly feel I am a Jew, and am proud of it... One needs something to believe in, something for which one can have whole hearted enthusiasm. One needs to feel that one's life has meaning, that one is needed in this world."[6]

Our community has suffered huge trauma and dislocation in the past two generations. Jewish communities face numerous modern day challenges, including assimilation and intermarriage. To triumph as a nation, modern Jewish women must draw from the knowledge imparted by this legacy of their ancestors throughout history.

Through intuitive understanding of others, unyielding dedication and innate communication skills, Jewish women have the tools to encourage and inspire all those around them in a manner which bestows dignity and confidence while still protecting their privacy.

The way ahead requires them to make considered choices about their bodies, their time and their desires. If they wish to develop their emotional, intellectual, physical and spiritual attributes then they, like our matriarchs, are blessed with the special skills and faith to make the right decisions.

Notes:

1 Deuteronomy 32.7
2 Midrash Tanchuma; Pinchas 7
3 Numbers 26:64, Rashi's comment
4 Midrash of Pirkei de Rabbi Eliezer, Parsha Ki Tissa
5 Hannah Senesh; Her Life and Diary; May 15th 1937
6 Ibid; October 27th, 1938

51 Have We Lost God in the Details?

Malcolm Herman

It is by all accounts a strange sight. A man is holding a lemon-like fruit in his hand at arms length. Slowly he rotates it 360 degrees, scrutinizing it intently. After a few moments he puts it down and picks up another to begin the process again. No, he is not from Agriculture and Fisheries checking quality in line with an obscure EU directive. He is standing, in fact, in a synagogue hall selecting an *etrog*. What makes it all the more bizarre is that this is the day after *Yom Kippur*. On Yom Kippur a Jew is supposed to attain unprecedented spiritual heights, commune with God and link with Jewish history – an elevating and edifying spiritual experience. Twenty four hours later, he is spot checking lemons.

Judaism appears to be preoccupied with details. Isn't religion about more lofty, esoteric practises? You know, meditation, spirituality, quite frankly, God!

Let's go back to Creation. The Torah is economical with words. In just thirty or so sentences we have the whole of Creation ex nihilo described, from planets to plants and everything in between.[1] In the book of Exodus, the construction of the *mishkan*, the mini temple, is discussed and we find *hundreds* of sentences devoted to every aspect of its design and construction.[2] The discrepancy can be addressed by an idea of Rabbi Samson Raphael Hirsch:

"To describe Judaism as a religion is to misrepresent what Judaism is. Religion is the thoughts of man about God. Judaism is the thoughts of God about man. In other religions there is interest in what things look like in heaven. In Judaism the focus is what they look like on earth." [3]

In other words, Judaism is not a 'religion', in the common usage of the term. In religion there is often a focus on the experiences which encourage people to transcend mundane life. But in Judaism the challenge is not only to *transcend* but also to *transform:* to bring God directly into everyday life, transforming us and life itself. It is to invest each moment and each opportunity with spirituality and sensitivity, from the most profound to the most prosaic.

The Biblical account of the history of Creation is humanity's attempt to grasp the otherworldly. It is an attempt to understand what God is. But that is not our primary focus, and so, is dispensed with in 30 verses. The building of the mishkan, however, is bringing "heaven down to earth", right into the centre of day-to-day existence. That is the essence of Judaism.

Of course, it goes without saying that there is also plenty of opportunity for deeply moving, spiritual moments – over *Shabbat*, through meaningful prayer, through study of Torah, through meditation – but these are not ends in themselves. The challenge really begins once these moments have passed; the challenge of moving from *transcendence* to *transformation*.

Broadly speaking, there are two ways to do this. These are our relationships between 'person and person' and between 'person and God'. Spiritual *maturity* is self-development in both areas. Spiritual *integrity* is consistency, from the first to the last, in public and in private, in macro and in micro.

It is to bring God through the front door, into the kitchen and the bedroom (*when you sit in your house*).[4] It is to have God in the passenger seat and in the office (*when you walk on the way*).[4] It is to weave the thread of otherworldliness through the day, from the first grouchy moments till your head hits the pillow (*when you wake and when you lie down*).[4]

It is true that some people do lose sight of the bigger picture. However, doing so is, without a doubt, to miss the mark. It is the details which are the means for bringing God into every aspect of everyday life.

Let's imagine you have had an exhilarating Yom Kippur (it can happen..!) You leave synagogue hungry but floating. You get into your car, switch on the ignition and hear a tap on the window. "Are you going my way?"

He knows full well that you are going in the opposite direction. You wring out a smile, invite your passenger in, only to discover that he also wants to make a quick stop first. (You know, one of those Jewish-style stop offs, "I'll only be a minute.") You are struggling to cope with this invasion of your spiritual reverie. You are also still hungry. By the time you arrive home, thoughts of spirituality have long been left behind.

But, if that is the case, you have missed the point. Judaism is supposed to transform us as human beings through to our core, and this means viewing the mundane act of giving someone a lift from the same spiritual perspective as prayer, because it is the detail, which brings God into our life.

Let's return to the beginning.

The loftiness of Yom Kippur is a starting point. Now we face the challenge of introducing God everywhere, so that there is no aspect devoid of God. We need to scrutinise, examine and spot check to be confident of consistency, both in our "person to person" and "person to God" relationships.

The etrog is a symbol of our heightened appreciation that in true Judaism the details do not obscure God. They reveal God. True, the etrog is a practice centred on "person and God" and in this article, we have not touched on the meaning of this *mitzvah* itself. But the instruction is clear. The secret of real, qualitative relationships lies in the minutiae. The Divine is *in* the detail.

Notes:
1 Genesis chapter 1.
2 Exodus chapters 25 – 28, and 35 – 40
3 Horeb (Soncino Press), introduction xlvi - xlix
4 Deuteronomy 6: 5-9

52 The Wonder of Creation

Richard Jacobs

One of the most remarkable places I've ever visited is the Iguazu falls on the Argentinian – Brazilian border. Before the plane prepares to land on the small clear stretch of land in this sub-tropical rainforest it flies over a breathtaking scene – a gigantic crescent of between 160 and 260 waterfalls (depending on the river level) 2,700 metres long and 80 metres high.

As you approach the falls on foot, one of the first things that strikes you (aside from the thunderous noise, heat and humidity) is the range of vegetation, and how foreign it looks. In fact there are more then 20,000 species of plants in the Iguazu region, approximately 8,000 of them found only in this one region. The behaviour of the animals near the falls is also remarkable. For example swifts spiral in the air hunting for insects by day until just before sunset when they gather in large numbers, their aeronautic skill and precision clearly identifiable as they dive through the curtain of falling water to roost on the rocks immediately behind.

There are approximately 1,413,000 known species in the world: of which 750,000 are insects and only 4,000 mammals. Over 100,000 of these insects are ants, bees and wasps. To put this in perspective, ant-life is responsible for 10% of the total animal biomass[1] worldwide, which dwarfs the humans, putting us into a minority category.

Why is there such a diversity of life? What purpose can it have? One answer could be the careful balance of the eco-system. The removal or introduction of even one species could have knock-on effect, potentially leading to the collapse of the entire system. This idea reflects Rabbinic teachings that a person's actions have a spiritual effect not only on the individual but also on the world at large. Torah sources add another perspective. The *Talmud*[2] tells us that not even one thing was created needlessly and gives examples of different animals which provide the source for medicinal cures.

In discussing how to fulfill the commandment to love God[3,] Maimonides offers what seem to be conflicting suggestions. On the one hand he states that this is achieved through the study of Torah.[4] On the other hand however, he writes elsewhere that contemplating the awe-inspiring wonders of the natural world leads one to love God.[5] These two statements appear to be contradictory; is the pathway to loving God through the physical or through the spiritual? The deeper Torah sources[6] tell us that there is no contradiction, because the Torah is the blueprint – the Architect's Plan – for the world; and as such, nature and the world around us are actually physical manifestations of the Torah.

There is however a crucial difference between using nature and using Torah as pathways to discovering God. A person could explore the natural world and discover the Divine[7], but equally they could reach the wrong conclusions. Two scientists can look through the lens of the same microscope but only one will see God's footprints. We are warned in several places of the danger of the fascination with nature, of seeing it as having created itself.[8] In fact the most ardent atheists are often those who specialise in the study of the natural world. Torah study however, is a reliable path to discovering (and coming to love) God. The complexity, the depth, the beauty is such that true study of Torah can lead a person in one direction only.

That said, we do have an obligation to thank God for the beauty He has placed in the world. The Sages instituted a number of blessings to be recited upon viewing natural wonders. For instance upon seeing such sights as majestic mountains, deserts and oceans, we recite the blessing: "Blessed are You God... who makes the work of creation." God has made a truly spectacular world for us and that is certainly something we should appreciate.

Of course, to simply go to an area of natural beauty like

Iguazu, look at the falls, foliage and fauna and declare "Ah! The wonder of creation!" is just the beginning. The real trick is to stop, look and listen. When we discover how a habitat or microclimate functions, investigate the millions of components that make up the organisms that live there, see how they interact, explore the complexity of intra and inter species communication, and consider the diversity and scope of animal behaviour we begin to better understand the nature of the world we live in. Then we can gain a real appreciation of the wonder of creation.

Notes:

1 The total weight of a particular group of organisms.

2 Babylonian Talmud Shabbat 77b

3 Deuteronomy 6:5

4 Maimonides, Sefer Hamitzvot, Positive Commandment 3

5 Maimonides, Hilchot Yisodei Hatorah 2:2

6 Midrash Bereshit Rabbah 1:1

7 E.g. Psalms 19, Psalms 104. It is interesting to note that the second half of psalm 19 extols the virtues of God's commandments, and the first half shows us how we can experience God's glory through nature.

8 E.g. Deuteronomy 4:19

53 From Vision to Reality

Zalman Noe

My wife and I are cousins. When we married we promised ourselves that we were going to rebuild whatever was destroyed by the Holocaust and bring up our children as committed Jews to restore all that we and the world had lost.

I was fifteen when I was sent to *Auschwitz*, after which I went to *Birkenau* and then to clear rubble in Warsaw. I spent those years in the presence of a remarkable man, Rabbi Yekutiel Yehuda Halberstam, the Sanz-Klausenberg Rebbe. In the Rebbe, you witnessed a man who had lost everything but never lost his faith, not even for one moment. When all that you have in the world is taken from you and you are stripped of all that you possess, when everything falls away, just the nature of the human being is left. This man had the vision to propel Jewish life and cause a rebirth of dynamic faith, trust, passion and courage. This is his story.

The Rebbe of the Klausenberg *Chassidim* tragically lost his wife and 11 children in Auschwitz. Throughout his brutal suffering and unfathomable torture in Auschwitz, the fire of his love for the Creator and his devotion to all Jews never wavered. He gave courage and hope in the depths of horror. "We will be liberated," he promised.

A survivor named Asher Brenner recalled, "In Auschwitz I was placed in the same group as the Rebbe. He suffered more than the rest of us because of his stubbornness. He refused to eat non-kosher food. He had managed to bring his tefillin into the camp with him, and he put them on every day. Notwithstanding great danger, he organised minyanim for prayer services. We often forgot about Shabbat completely, but the Rebbe avoided desecrating Shabbat every week and made sure that no one else did the work that was imposed on him.

All this drew the attention of the Kapos, and they punished the Rebbe with vicious beatings. But slowly a change in attitude took place amongst them. Looking at him with new respect, they started to treat him more kindly. They came to recognize the Rebbe's unique character, principles and total devotion to God."[1]

After the destruction of Warsaw in 1944, the Rebbe was amongst the 5,000 frail survivors led on a brutal death march toward *Dachau*. It was on this march, barefoot and fasting in the heat of the summer on *Tisha B'Av*, that the Rebbe was shot in the arm for attempting to escape. Pulling wet leaves off a tree, he bandaged his wound and rejoined the march. It was at this moment he vowed that if he survived these atrocities, no matter how profound his physical and emotional loss, he would one day build a hospital that would be dedicated to treating people with loving kindness and preserving the sanctity, dignity and physical well being of all people.

The Rebbe then devoted himself completely to reviving Jews who emerged from the camps and restoring them to a vibrant Jewish life. Hidden strengths, leadership and resourcefulness suddenly awakened within him. He rekindled the spirit within each Jew he met, calling out with a clear and confident voice, "He who is for God, come to me!"

An [unobservant] Jew was once standing near the Rebbe in Auschwitz and overheard him explaining the verse from Psalms, "Sing to God a new song for He has performed amazing feats. His right hand and holy arm have helped Him."

"I did not understand what he was saying," recalled the man, "but the verse enraged me. Where were God's amazing feats? Where was His outstretched arm? Many years and life experiences later, however, I recalled the explanation that the Klausenberger Rebbe had given and the idea entered my mind — wasn't that in and of itself an amazing feat? In the hell of Auschwitz there was a Jew who was still faithful to the Almighty and took strength in the amazing feats that He had promised to perform in the future. This thought caused me, late in my life, to begin to return to our faith."[2]

In the Displaced Person Camps, after liberation, the Rebbe breathed new life into the broken-hearted and healed their physical and spiritual wounds, caring for thousands of lonely orphans who had no one left in the world. He fought against the oppressive hopelessness which gripped survivors and he organised men, women and children in the camps into genuine, traditional Jewish communities. Networks of *yeshivot* for girls and boys flourished in the camps. The Rebbe's main emphasis was restoring the institution of Jewish marriage, assisting *agunot* to remarry and raising the necessary funds to provide the basic needs for every bride and groom.

His warmth and intense love for the Jewish people inspired the growth of new communities throughout New York, Canada, Mexico, Chile and Israel. In his forties, the Rebbe moved to Israel and, against all political and geographical odds, established a thriving Jewish community in Netanya.

The foundation stone for Laniado Hospital was laid in 1975. At the ground-breaking ceremony of the first department, which was maternity, he emotionally proclaimed to those assembled, "I can hear the cries of the babies who will be born here." It was this accomplishment that he believed would open the gates of new life for all people, regardless of religion or race. More than any of his yeshivot, schools, housing projects, orphanages and synagogues, this particular enterprise fulfilled his dream. He said, "If the yeshivot are likened to the holy area of the Temple, then the hospital will be considered the *Holy of Holies*."

Encouraged by the belief that he was saved for the purpose of saving others, he built Laniado, where medicine would be practiced with compassion and sympathy — an institution where healing is administered at the hands of highly trained professionals who exemplify the Jewish tradition of caring for others. He developed a set of founding principles to guide the operation of the hospital focusing on the holistic needs of the patient. This includes the belief that "Every effort shall be made to relieve the physical suffering of all patients and uplift their mental outlook in order to provide them with the best overall therapeutic treatment." This tenet still overrides all other priorities and demands.

In keeping with Rabbi Halberstam's legacy, in 2004, Laniado opened a Children's Hospital in memory of the 1.5 million children who perished in the Holocaust. The sustaining flame of his passion to rebuild the world despite all that had happened to him fuels every nurse, doctor and member of staff who works at Laniado. They are one family united by a vision that they continually strive to achieve.

The Rebbe was all too familiar with the tragedy of the Holocaust. But he did not despair. Instead, he kept on living and bringing others back to life. In building Laniado, he endowed the Jewish people with a legacy of humanity. This has created a link between the millions of children our people lost and the millions of children who will now become our future.

Notes:

1 *The Klausenberger Rebbe: The War Years,* Targum Press
2 Ibid.

54 Private Winneger

Kalman Packousz

Young Private Winneger was with the US army as it marched through Europe at the end of World War II. His unit was assigned to a European village with orders to secure the town, search for any hiding Nazis and help the villagers in any way they could.

Winneger was on patrol one night when he saw a figure running through a field just outside the village. He shouted, "Halt or I'll shoot!" The figure ducked behind a tree. Winneger waited and eventually the figure came out. Assuming that Winneger was no longer nearby, the figure started to dig a hole in the ground. Winneger waited until the figure had finished digging and had begun to move. Winnegar stepped out and again shouted, "Halt or I'll shoot!" The figure began to run. Despite himself, Winneger decided not to shoot, but instead to catch the furtive figure. He soon caught up with the fleeing fugitive and tackled him to the ground.

To his surprise, he found that he had captured a young boy. An ornate *menorah* had fallen from the boy's hands during the scuffle. Winneger picked it up. The boy tried to grab it back, shouting, "Give it to me. It's mine!" Winneger assured the boy that he was among friends and that he himself was Jewish.

The boy had just survived several years in a concentration camp, and was mistrustful of all men in uniform. He had been forced to watch helplessly as his father was shot and had no idea what had became of his mother.

In the weeks that followed Winneger took the young boy, who was called David, under his wing. As they gradually became close, Winneger offered David the opportunity to return with him to New York City. David agreed, and having processed all the necessary paperwork, Winneger officially adopted him.

Winneger was active in the New York Jewish community. An acquaintance of his, a curator of the Jewish Museum in Manhattan, saw the menorah. With great excitement, he told David that it was an extremely valuable and historic menorah which should be available to the entire Jewish community. The curator offered David $50,000 for the menorah, a huge sum in the post-war years. But David refused any offer. The menorah had been passed down as a family heirloom for over two hundred years. Especially after his suffering in the Holocaust, no amount of money would make him part with the menorah.

When *Chanukah* came, David and Winneger lit the menorah in the front window of their home in New York City. David went upstairs to his room to study, while Winneger stayed downstairs, gazing at the menorah. Suddenly, there was a knock on the door. When Winneger went to answer it, he found a woman who spoke with a strong German accent. She said that she had been walking down the street and saw the menorah in the window. Once there had been one just like it in her family and she had never seen another like it since. Could she come in and get a closer look, she asked?

Winneger invited her in, saying that the menorah belonged to his son, who would explain its history. He called to David to come and talk to the woman – but David had no need to speak about the menorah. In fact, he was too shocked to speak at all, for this woman was his mother.

Three thousand miles away from the destruction of Europe, the menorah's sparks of hope twinkled alongside the elation of a long lost mother who had just been reunited with her son.

55 Freedom of Will

Saul Zneimer

One of the most intractable philosophical problems that Judaism has to deal with, is the issue of freedom of will.

On the one hand, we take for granted the principle that God knows everything. Whatever we do, whatever happens in the world, not only does He know about it, He knew it before it happened. On the other hand, we operate with the principle that man is a free agent, able to make his own choices.

According to the principle of God's foreknowledge, God knew what choice would be made before it was made. Yet the concept of personal choice tells us that different options could have been taken. Both God and man are impacted by this dilemma.

How can we say of God that, in some way, He did not really know? Are we prepared to limit His understanding of the future? As the *Rambam* says, "God either knows in advance that this person will be righteous or wicked, or He does not know. If He knows, then it is impossible that he will not be (wicked)....And if you say ...it is possible that he should be wicked...then God does not know the future with certainty."[1] God's foreknowledge does not seem to allow space for freedom of will.

What then will we say about man's freedom to choose? Not only does God's knowledge seem to limit our ability to choose, it also encroaches on the idea of responsibility and accountability. How can a person be held accountable for actions if they were pre-ordained? How could that possibly be fair? Moreover, how could a just God ever punish us for our mistakes, or indeed reward us for our *mitzvot*? If all we can do, is follow the script preconfigured in God's mind, reward and punishment become not only unfair, but unjust.

Any attempt to understand the nature of God, to understand

the infinite from a finite perspective, is by definition only to be able to grasp with our fingertips, the beginnings of the answer. In fact, *Rabbi Akiva* stated the simple Jewish response when he said, fully aware of the dilemma, "Everything is foreseen, yet freedom is given" and Rambam himself concludes by saying that this is an unknowable concept.

We are nevertheless required to live and work within this impossible contradiction, and the commentators over time, have therefore offered various insights to apply to this paradox from our perspective.

Saadia Gaon and *Yehuda HaLevi* argued that in some way time is reversed for God. Normally, a cause precedes and leads to an effect. In our question, given what God is, His knowledge is not the cause of our actions, but the result. When we freely choose to do an action therefore, God has already known in the past. This is a difficult concept to grasp.

An analogy to this has been suggested by Chief Rabbi Dr Jonathan Sacks. Imagine viewing a video-recording of a football match you already watched live. The goal is the same. The player's choice to shoot to the left or to the right is unchanged. Does your knowing the result impact in any way on that shot's delivery? No, of course it does not. In the game itself, the choice to shoot left or right existed. God's knowledge might be said to be like the video, the 'past' as it were caused by the 'future', but nevertheless not having an impact on it.

A second approach is taken by the mystics who argued that God withdrew himself from the world He created, in order to leave a space for man to act freely. In some way, God allowed himself not to have any impact on our moral choices, giving us freedom, and thus responsibility, for our own actions. Moreover, others point out, it is this ability to make choices without apparent cause, that lies at the core of our being. It is a function of our souls and is how we are most able to emulate God, who Himself is, of course, totally beyond control. This argument conjures up an image of an all powerful, omniscient God who chooses to limit His impact to allow us to grow and fulfil our potential.

Rambam asserts forcefully that man has free will. He explores various dimensions of the issue and stresses the importance of the question, without underestimating its difficulty. "Know," he says, "that the answer to this question is longer than the earth and wider than the sea and many great and important principles depend on it." [2] His answer is to argue that the way God knows things is different from the way humans do. This, too, is extremely difficult for us to grasp.

To quote another analogy, again from the Chief Rabbi, it may be understood as similar to the way a parent knows a child. A mother may be able to predict infallibly how her son/daughter will react, because of a deep intuitive understanding of the child. The child and the mother are separate people but she 'knows' about him by way of insight. On this basis, one might suggest that God, as our Creator, 'knows' what we will do – intrinsically.

The Torah itself is adamant, both that we have freedom to make choices and that God wants us to exercise our will for the good. "I call Heaven and Earth today, to bear witness: I have placed life and death before you, blessing and curse; and you shall choose Life." [3]

All our thinkers concur though, that we not only are we free to choose, but that we are responsible for the choices we make and that furthermore, the Torah gives us the information we need to make the right choices. Ultimately therefore our role is not to understand God, but to understand ourselves and the Torah, in order to live life to the full.

Notes:
1 Hilchot Teshuva 5:5
2 Ibid
3 Deuteronomy: 30:19

56 Spirituality Without God

Sara Rigler

Melody died last week, at the age of forty-two. Exactly 12 months ago, she got a surprise diagnosis: that her throbbing back pains were caused by metastasised breast cancer.

Her prognosis was less than two months to live. Melody and her long-time boyfriend Kevin fought valiantly, using every weapon in the arsenal of New Age cures including energy healing, acupuncture, rebirthing, visualisation, diet, and contact with nature, in addition to radiation and chemotherapy.

Although I did not know Melody well, her ordeal touched me deeply. She had been a periodic member of the ashram where I lived for 15 years before moving to Jerusalem and taking on the path of Judaism. The daughter of a Swedenborgian minister, Melody practiced a generic New Age religion, which embraced meditation, vibrational healing, positive thinking, and music. She played the guitar and sang beautiful songs of her own composition, songs about love and the spirit.

Kevin sent out frequent e-mails about Melody's progress, and eventual decline. In the spring she rallied, miraculously defying her prognosis. She started to walk again, gained weight, and was featured on a PBS television special about alternative healing. A euphoric Kevin wrote to thank all the people who had sent Melody their prayers and healing thoughts.

Something was bothering me. I wondered why, in his long letter, he never thanked God.

Throughout the year, Kevin wrote of angels, miracles, spiritual worlds, dreams, and the importance of sending Melody only positive energy. Many times he asked everyone to pray, but the more I contemplated his messages, the more I became aware of something I can only call, "horizontal prayer" the sending of positive, healing wishes for recovery not to God, but to Melody! In fact, in his very first letter Kevin wrote:

"I've asked that all the Swedenborgian churches that we performed at during the Peace Prayer tour offer prayers to Melody this Sunday morning."

I originally thought the "to" was a typo.

The last letter, written by Devipriya, one of our ashram friends, described Melody's passing, she was surrounded by fragrant flowers, with four of the ashram members chanting to their lineage of gurus, sending her off to complete her mission in the spirit world. During the transition, they devotedly followed the directions of a shaman and a Buddhist lama. Devipriya wrote: "The room was so charged and so peaceful at the same time, like angels had come and lifted her from her body."

God was never mentioned.

Reading that letter amidst my sorrow, I couldn't help but think how different is the focus of the Jewish tradition, where a yearning for a connection with God permeates every conscious act.

My Rabbi is fond of saying: "Judaism is not a religion, it's a relationship." All the elements of Judaism work to further the relationship between the human being and God. Prayer is vertical; a one-to-one conversation with God. The commandments are to be performed in the same way that a lover does the bidding of his or her beloved. Therefore, Judaism without God would be like *Romeo and Juliet* without Juliet.

It is a truism that increasing numbers of people are not marrying, because of their inability to commit to a relationship. One wonders if the predilection for spirituality without God derives from the same syndrome: valuing freedom and independence over a relationship which will often demand the total giving of one's self.

My teacher says that even when one is dealing with a situation in accordance with lofty principles and techniques, one must still ask, "Is God in the picture?"

For example, the self-help market offers dozens of books on how to control destructive anger. All these techniques may be useful. Judaism, however, would add that when faced with an anger-provoking situation, one must recognize that *everything* comes from God. And that includes the phone ringing with a wrong number in the middle of the night, the spilled salad dressing on your just-washed floor, the train you are running to catch pulling out of the station one minute early. No matter which techniques you apply to bring down your blood pressure, if God is not in the picture, you are missing out on a custom-made opportunity to connect with the Divine.

What's wrong with a picture devoid of God? Quite simply, God is reality, both ultimate reality and immediate reality. To live in this world oblivious to God is like being a fish oblivious to water. It's okay for a fish, but not for a person who aspires to greater consciousness.

After two centuries engrossed in a materialistic vision of the world, the West is enjoying a resurgence of spirituality. The popularity of angels, psychic phenomena, faith healing, meditation, and near-death experiences testifies to a paradigm shift in our concept of reality. We have at long last begun to recognise that reality includes a spiritual dimension, which is not susceptible to scientific measurement.

But somehow God has gotten lost in the shuffle. It is rather like a lavish *Bar Mitzvah* party, replete with a 10-piece orchestra, 14 tables of smorgasbord, six Viennese dessert tables, a troupe of jugglers and acrobats, and no glimpse of the Bar Mitzvah boy.

The materialistic worldview which prevailed in the 19th and 20th centuries denied the existence of God. The spiritual worldview gaining popularity at the threshold of the 21st century is too busy with psychic phenomena and personal growth to care about the existence of God.

It is no coincidence that the most popular Eastern paths in the West are derivatives of Buddhism, a non-theistic religion. Gautama Buddha, the fifth century BCE founder of Buddhism, never mentioned God in his teachings. His Four

Noble Truths and his Eightfold Way speak about escaping the inherent suffering of this world by transcending desire and practicing right action and thought. The entire thrust is on human consciousness, control of mind, and self effort. This forms the prototype of most of the personal growth movements prevalent in America.

While Hinduism is a totally theistic religion, its American transplants emphasise their lineage of gurus rather than the deities of the Hindu pantheon (with the exception of the Krishna Consciousness movement).

The advantages of spirituality without God are obvious: one can choose one's own direction, methods, and goals without the intrusions of the Divine. The 'inner voice,' which functions as the CEO of most New Age enterprises, rarely tells one what one doesn't want to hear.

Judaism, on the other hand, has bequeathed to the world a God who not only created and sustains the universe, but who commanded us, "Do not steal," and, "Do not commit adultery." Little wonder that most people resist such encroachments to their personal lives. Of course Judaism isn't just about the limitations, and to view it as such is to strip it of its essence: that of putting together piece by piece, the picture that allows human beings to connect to Infinity.

Yes there are disciplines, but behind each one, behind each positive action or restriction there is an Ultimate Purpose. Can there be anything more meaningful to life?

57 End of Days

Daniel Rowe

Belief in a messianic end to history forms one of the beliefs which are classified in the Torah tradition as fundamental. So fundamental, in fact, that denial of it is a rejection of the entire system of Torah tradition. Why is this so? Why is it not sufficient to believe in an afterlife, to believe that there is ultimate justice? What does the belief in a messiah and a Messianic era add to a Jew's existence?

Furthermore, the *Rambam* states that although we fully believe in a messianic end, we cannot know what it will be like. Even the prophecies we have concerning the arrival of the Messiah, will only be properly understood in retrospect. How can there be meaning in believing in an end which we cannot fathom? A dream absent of content can hardly be a meaningful dream, let alone lay the foundation of an entire thought system!

Yet Jew after Jew went to their torturous death, their dying words reaffirming this unshakable commitment to the conviction that there will yet come an age of perfection; a climactic crescendo to the tumultuousness of history. As if this ungraspable end would somehow justify their own deaths now.

This latter paradox can, in fact, be found within the Torah itself. As Jacob is dying, "… [he] called to his children, saying, 'come that I may reveal to you that which will occur at the End of Days.'" Yet as we read on, the great revelation is not forthcoming. The *Gemara* tells us that Jacob indeed sought to prophetically reveal the End of Days, but at the expectant moment he found no vision. At first, he assumed that it was a suspension of prophecy, perhaps due to some of his family being unworthy recipients, but he soon realised instead that the fault lay not in the circumstances of the prophecy, but in its essential content. For the End of Days simply cannot be revealed! That is a part of its essence! And herein lay the first clue as to the mystery of world history itself.

The end cannot be revealed for it is not a fixed vision awaiting actualisation. It is, rather, an outgrowth of all that precedes it. Just as a seed decaying in the ground, long detached from its life-giving source confounds us with the sudden appearance of shoots and eventually a full living plant; and just as the torturous path of labour suddenly gives way to full blown life; so too the 'birth-pangs' of history, the rot and decay of society, the hopelessness of it all... suddenly give way to the most remarkable growth and development, to pure life itself! And in their doing so, we see revealed that there never was a contradiction.

In the dawning awareness, the observer cannot but be overwhelmed by an awe of the process that appeared so death-like, and yet was all along step-by-step delivering the life within. It is no coincidence, therefore, that the prayer for the Messianic end refers to the 'seed of David sprouting forth'!

Understood correctly, the end provides a whole new perspective on all that came before, all that seemed so dark...

The pattern can be seen at each stage of Jewish history. In the *Purim* story world Jewry is hopelessly pitted against an irrevocable decree to annihilate them in their entirety; a time so hopelessly dark, exhibiting no sign of hope. God Himself shows no overt presence – His name is not even mentioned in the biblical book that records this dramatic story! The Persian king is hopelessly swayed by the opinion of others, incapable of taking matters into his own hands; the closet-Jewish Queen Esther is legally forbidden from approaching the king unbidden; the Jewish people lie hopelessly at the mercy of the one man with any real power, the advisor-come-deputy, the de facto ruler, the arch anti-Semite – Haman. A world so dark that God Himself is not revealed. A seed fallen. Death-pangs.

Yet as Jewry watches, hopeless, there appears a shocking reversal. The forces of anti-Jew, of anti-God themseves end up producing their own destruction! All that seemed so dark not only makes way for the light, but reveals that all along it was capable of nothing else! Haman was destroyed by his own decree! Unbeknown to him his 'final solution' had implicated the Queen, whose national identity had hitherto remained concealed! Yet it was none other than Haman himself whose elaborate scheming had seen to it that she become queen! A seed of salvation hidden indeed! A queen whose very name is 'concealment' (Esther)! Haman's own laws had conspired to destroy him, save world Jewry, and in doing so reveal the tremendous Hand guiding history all along. And of course, how fitting that Haman's end was met on the very gallows that he himself had constructed for Mordechai!

In Jewish consciousness it is the Purim story that serves as the perfect example of all of world history. Purim, the very name of the festival, means 'randomness' and is derived from Haman himself. Yet that day now celebrates the irony that apparent chaos can produce nothing but order. Haman it is, in the end, who shows most decisively *ein od milevado* – that there is nothing but God! All that appears to the contrary is a mask, for the end will inevitably reveal the life that lay within all along. The Jew celebrates, wearing the mask of history, and drinks to a consciousness that reveals that as far as history is concerned there is no ultimate difference between the pathway of Haman and that of Mordechai!

Thus understood, belief in a Messianic delivery is, in fact, belief in history itself. All pathways *must* lead to the climactic revelation, yet it is we who decide which pathway history takes – the way of Mordechai or the long, painful way of Haman. We must therefore, at one and the same time, believe that history has an end, a goal *and* that the end is unknowable at present – because it is up to us. We are now able to view ourselves and our daily struggles as nothing less than an act of partnership in the breathtaking fabric of creation itself; thereby giving meaning to every trial every tragedy, – something so fundamental, so inspiring, so empowering.

58 A Prayer

By Elie Wiesel

Master of the Universe, let us make up. It is time. How long can we go on being angry?

More than 50 years have passed since the nightmare was lifted. Many things, good and less good, have since happened to those who survived it. They learned to build on ruins. Family life was re-created. Children were born, friendships struck. They learned to have faith in their surroundings, even in their fellow men and women. Gratitude has replaced bitterness in their hearts. No one is as capable of thankfulness as they are. Thankful to anyone willing to hear their tales and become their ally in the battle against apathy and forgetfulness. For them every moment is grace.

Oh, they do not forgive the killers and their accomplices, nor should they. Nor should You, Master of the Universe. But they no longer look at every passer-by with suspicion. Nor do they see a dagger in every hand.

Does this mean that the wounds in their soul have healed? They will never heal. As long as a spark of the flames of *Auschwitz* and *Treblinka* glows in their memory, so long will my joy be incomplete.

What about my faith in You, Master of the Universe? I now realise I never lost it, not even over there, during the darkest hours of my life. I don't know why I kept on whispering my daily prayers, and those reserved for the *Shabbat*, and for the holidays, but I did recite them, often with my father and on *Rosh Hashanah* eve, with hundreds of inmates at Auschwitz. Was it because the prayers remained a link to the vanished world of my childhood?

But my faith was no longer pure. How could it be? It was filled with anguish rather than fervor, with perplexity more than piety. In the kingdom of eternal night, on the Days of Awe, which are the Days of Judgment, my traditional prayers were directed to You as well as against You, Master of the

Universe. What hurt me more: Your absence or Your silence?

In my testimony I have written harsh words, burning words about Your role in our tragedy. I would not repeat them today. But I felt them then. I felt them in every cell of my being. Why did You allow, if not enable, the killer day after day, night after night to torment, kill and annihilate tens of thousands of Jewish children? Why were they abandoned by Your Creation? These thoughts were in no way destined to diminish the guilt of the guilty. Their established culpability is irrelevant to my "problem" with You, Master of the Universe. In my childhood I did not expect much from human beings. But I expected everything from You.

Where were You, God of kindness, in Auschwitz? What was going on in heaven, at the celestial tribunal, while Your children were marked for humiliation, isolation and death only because they were Jewish?

These questions have been haunting me for more than six decades. You have vocal defenders, You know. Many theological answers were given to me, such as: "God is God. He alone knows what He is doing. One has no right to question Him or His ways." Or: "Auschwitz was a punishment for European Jewry's sins of assimilation." And: "Isn't Israel the solution? Without Auschwitz, there would have been no Israel."

I reject all these answers. Auschwitz must and will forever remain a question mark only: it can be conceived neither with God nor without God. At one point, I began wondering whether I was not unfair with You. After all, Auschwitz was not something that came down ready-made from heaven. It was conceived by men, implemented by men, staffed by men. And their aim was to destroy not only us but You as well. Ought we not to think of Your pain, too? Watching your children suffer at the hands of Your other children, haven't you also suffered?

When we as Jews enter the High Holidays, preparing ourselves to pray for a year of peace and happiness for our people and all people, let us make up, Master of the Universe. In spite of everything that happened? Yes, in spite. Let us make up, for the child in me, it is unbearable to be divorced from You for so long.

Reprinted with permission from New York Times. October 2nd 1997

59 Why Am I a Jew?

Chief Rabbi Dr Jonathan Sacks

Why am I a Jew? Not because I believe that the Jews represent all there is of the human story. Jews didn't write Shakespeare's sonnets or Beethoven's quartets. We did not give the world the serene beauty of a Japanese garden or the architecture of ancient Greece. Whilst I love these things, they are not ours.

Nor am I a Jew because of anti-Semitism or to avoid giving Hitler a posthumous victory. What happens to me does not define who I am: ours is a people of faith, not fate. Nor is it because I think that Jews are better than other people; more intelligent, virtuous, law-abiding, creative, generous or successful. The difference lies not in Jews but in Judaism, not in what we are but in what we are called on to be.

I am a Jew because, being a child of my people, I have heard the call to add my chapter to its unfinished story. I am a stage on its journey, a connected link between the generations. The dreams and hopes of my ancestors live on in me, and I am the guardian of their trust, now and for the future.

I am a Jew because our ancestors were the first to see that the world is driven by a moral purpose, that reality is not a ceaseless war of the elements, to be worshipped as gods, nor history a battle in which might is right and power is to be appeased. The Judaic tradition shaped the moral civilisation of the West, teaching for the first time that human life is sacred, that the individual may not be sacrificed for the mass, and that rich and poor, great and small, are all equal before God.

I am a Jew because I am the moral heir of those who stood at the foot of Mount Sinai and pledged themselves to live by these truths, becoming a kingdom of priests and a holy nation. I am the descendant of countless generations of ancestors, who though sorely tested and bitterly tried, remained faithful to that covenant when they might so easily have defected.

I am a Jew because of *Shabbat*, the world's greatest religious institution, a time in which there is no manipulation of nature or our fellow human beings, in which we come together in freedom and equality to create, every week, an anticipation of the Messianic age.

I am a Jew because our nation, though at times it suffered the deepest poverty, never gave up on its commitment to helping the poor, or rescuing Jews from the other lands, or fighting for justice for the oppressed, and did so without self-congratulation, because it was a *mitzvah*, because a Jew could do no less.

I am a Jew because I cherish the Torah, knowing that God is to be found not in natural forces but in moral meanings, in words, texts, teachings and commands, and because Jews, though they may have lacked all else, never ceased to value education as a sacred task, endowing the individual with dignity and depth.

I am a Jew because of our people's passionate faith in freedom, holding that each of us is a moral agent, and that in this lies our unique dignity as human beings; and because Judaism never left its ideals at the level of lofty aspirations, but instead translated them into deeds, that we call *mitzvot*, and a way, which we call the *halachah*, and thus brought heaven down to earth.

I am proud, simply, to be a Jew.

I am proud to be part of a people who, though scarred and traumatised, never lost their humour or their faith, their ability to laugh at present troubles and still believe in ultimate redemption; who saw human history as a journey, and never stopped travelling and searching.

I am proud to be part of an age in which my people, ravaged by the worst crime ever to be committed against a people, responded by reviving a land, recovering their sovereignty, rescuing threatened Jews throughout the world, rebuilding Jerusalem and proving themselves to be as courageous in the pursuit of peace as in defending themselves in war.

I am proud that our ancestors refused to be satisfied with

premature consolations, and in answer to the question, "Has the Messiah come?" always answered, "Not yet."

I am proud to belong to the people of Israel, whose name means "one who wrestles with God and with man and prevails." For though we have loved humanity, we have never stopped wrestling with it, challenging the idols of every age. And though we have loved God with an everlasting love, we have never stopped wrestling with Him nor He with us.

And though I admire other civilisations, and believe each has brought something special into the world, still this is my people and my heritage. In our uniqueness lies our universality. Through being what we alone are, we give to humanity what only we can give.

This then, is our story, our gift to the next generation. I received it from my parents and they from theirs across great expanses of space and time. There is nothing quite like it. It challenged, and today it still challenges the moral imagination of mankind. I want to say to my children: "Take it, cherish it, learn to understand and to love it. Carry it, and it will carry you. And you may in turn pass it onto your children. For you are a member of an eternal people, a letter in their scroll. Let their eternity live on in you."

60 60 Days for 60 Years

Andrew Shaw

60 days ago, you embarked on a period of commemoration. A positive memorial both for you and for the person in whose memory you have learned. 60 days later, it is hoped that each individual involved in the project has a greater understanding of their Judaism today and the role they want to play in the next 60 years.

For those who started their 60 days on the 25th January 2005 today is *Purim*, the happiest day in the Jewish calendar, and it is no coincidence that the project ends today. Purim is a day when we remember our victory against the odds, against an age old Hitler – *Haman*. It was a time when it seemed that the Jews were destined for imminent destruction. Miraculously we survived, to defeat Haman, then, as now, to return to Israel to rebuild our homeland.

Sixty years ago who would have believed there could be any positive future for the Jewish people? Communities had been wiped out, synagogues destroyed, hundreds of years of Jewish life eradicated as if they had never existed, and six million of our people had been lost.

However, just as we did in days of old, we rebuilt. From the ashes of the Holocaust came the State of Israel, communities were recreated and the vibrancy that had been part of our history began to return. Now, as we stand at the beginning of a new century we can marvel at how far we have come in those sixty years.

Purim is a day to rejoice in our achievements, to hear the Book of Esther being read and to drown out Haman's name. It is a time to give gifts to each other, as well as to charity and to hold a festive meal of joyous abandon. This Purim we have even more to celebrate – remembering our past whilst celebrating the finishing of this book and the start of further exploration into the fascinating world of Judaism.

In one month it will be *Pesach*. As you sit around your Pesach table and hear the same four questions that you have heard every year, ask yourself a few more. What have I achieved? And more importantly, what now? The first question is easy, you have taken upon yourself the monumental task of learning in memory of a person who didn't have the opportunity, taking an individual who had been reduced to a "number" and making them human again. The second question is a challenge that faces all of us.

There is a custom in Judaism to have a *siyum* – a celebratory meal – upon the finishing of a piece of Jewish learning. The most common siyum is made upon finishing a tractate of *Talmud*. The two words that we say after we have completed the tractate are two Aramaic words, 'hadran alach', which means, 'we shall return to you'. There is a powerful message here, as soon as a Jew finishes his learning, he vows to return to his learning, to continue the journey, to not rest on his laurels.

60 days ago we began this project together, we have studied together, we have remembered together. Now, as we end the book, as we end the project we should collectively say 'hadran alach' we shall return to you. We have only given a taste of each topic; it is not possible to distil all the wisdom of Judaism into 60 essays, it is for all of us to take the studying further. That, I believe, is our challenge.

Thank you for taking part in a project which I hope has been a fitting commemoration to those who lost their lives over 60 years ago. I will finish with the words of the Chief Rabbi which opened this book. "If each of us in the coming year makes a significant personal gesture to show that Judaism is alive and being lived, there can be no more momentous signal to humanity that evil does not have the final victory, because *Am Yisrael Chai*, the Jewish people lives."

Looking to the future

Photo courtesy of the State of Israel National Photo Collection

19. *Child leaving a Displaced Persons camp - 11 July 1945.* The eight year old Israel Meir Lau, survivor of Buchenwald and future Chief Rabbi of Israel beginning a new life.

20. *Thousands of Jews at the Western Wall in Jerusalem on Succot.*

21. *The flag of Israel flies at half mast in memory of the 6 million.*
Remembering the past. Building the future.

For suggested further reading or for websites on the topics discussed in this book visit www.tribeuk.com

If you have any feedback on the 60 Days for 60 Years project, please email us at info@tribeuk.com

Biographies

Chief Rabbi Dr Jonathan Sacks: Chief Rabbi of the United Hebrew Congregations of the Commonwealth since September 1, 1991. Widely recognised as one of the world's leading contemporary exponents of Judaism. A gifted communicator, the Chief Rabbi is a frequent contributor to radio, television and the national press. Each year before Rosh Hashanah he delivers a message to the British nation on BBC Television. He is also the author of thirteen books.

Chief Rabbi Warren Goldstein: Chief Rabbi of South Africa. Co-author of "African Soul Talk" with Dumani Mandela, a dialogue on the values for the new South Africa. An advocate of the High Court of South Africa.

Rabbi Dr Abraham Twerski: Descended from a long and distinguished Rabbinic ancestry. Recognized as an international authority in the chemical dependency field, he is also a resident psychiatrist, and an Associate Professor of Psychiatry. A prolific author, he has written 44 books to date on topics such as stress, self-esteem, spirituality and drug and alcohol dependencies. Appears frequently as a radio and television guest, and has received the Martin Luther King Citizen's Award.

Rabbi Dr Akiva Tatz: Qualified as a Doctor in South Africa. Was an army medical officer on the Namibian border during the conflict there. Studied in yeshiva in Jerusalem and founded the Jerusalem Medical Ethics Forum. Author of books on Jewish philosophy which have been translated into six languages. Currently a senior lecturer at the JLE – London.

Rabbi Paysach J Krohn: A fifth generation Mohel, affiliated with major hospitals in NY. Author of a book on Brit Milah, six "Maggid" books and 500 stories, and has a series of 80 tapes.

Rabbi Jonathan Dove: Holds a Masters Degree in Psychotherapy and Counselling, and has a private practice in psychotherapy. He is a member of the Chief Rabbi's

Cabinet, with Portfolio for Drugs and Mental Health. Former Jewish Student Chaplain based in Leeds and London. Established Nefesh U.K. the Network of Orthodox Mental Health Professionals.

Gerald Schroeder: Author and lecturer, PhD from M.I.T. where he taught for seven years. Has witnessed the detonation of six atom bombs. Currently teaches Science and the Bible at Aish HaTorah in Jerusalem. GS@geraldschroeder.com

Rabbi Gideon Sylvester: Studied history at Birmingham University, holds a Masters in Philosophy of Education from London University. Former Rabbi of Radlett United Synagogue. Recently made aliyah to Israel.

Dr James Weiss: Associate Professor of Education at Manhattan College NY.

Rabbi Dr Jeffrey Cohen: Currently Senior Rabbi of the Stanmore and Canons Park Synagogue. Educated in Yeshiva and Jews' College, and gained an MA from London University and a doctorate from the University of Glasgow. Former Director of Jewish Education in Manchester, the author of some 15 books and 300 articles.

Rabbi Simon Jacobson: Renowned lecturer and author of the best-selling book 'Toward a Meaningful Life' which has sold over 300,000 copies world wide. Founder and Director of The Meaningful Life Centre

Rabbi Shmuel Arkush: Studied in Yeshivot in the UK, Israel and America and worked as a Jewish Student Chaplain. Founder and Director of Operation Judaism which works to educate and support individuals who have become involved in missionary activity. www.operationjudaism.org

Rabbi Tzvi Freeman: Involved at an early age in Tao and radical politics, then left a career as a guitarist and composer to study Talmud and Jewish mysticism for nine years. Author of 'Bringing Heaven Down to Earth' as well as 'Daily Dose of Wisdom'. Consultant and lecturer in the field of educational technology.

Holly Pavlov: Jewish educator and author. Founder

and director of She'arim, College of Jewish Studies for Women in Jerusalem.

Rabbi Jeremy Conway: Executive Director of the United Synagogue London Beth Din Kashrut Division and the Director of the United Synagogue Religious Affairs Group. Formerly the Rabbi of the Beis Hamedrash Hagadol Synagogue in Leeds and a former London Jewish Student Chaplain.

Yaffa Eliach: Born in Lithuania. A Holocaust survivor. Professor of Literature at Brooklyn College NY and founder and Director of the Centre for Holocaust Studies. She is a poet and playwright and has received many awards for Holocaust related issues.

Yitta Halberstam: Authored eight books, including six in the 'Small Miracles' series. The first volume *Small Miracles* was a national bestseller in the United States, appearing on major bestseller lists, including *The New York Times* and *USA Today*. She has appeared on many radio and television shows, and two stories from *Small Miracles* were featured on the Oprah Winfrey Show. ymye@aol.com

Dayan Yonatan Abraham: Dayan of the London Beth Din, Former Rabbi to a community in Melbourne, Australia. Rabbinic consultant for Tribe.

Rabbi Moshe Krupka is the Executive Director of Programmes for the Orthodox Union, covering The United States and Canada.

Rabbi YY Rubinstein: Regular broadcaster on National BBC TV & Radio. Regularly writes for *HaModia* and teacher at Seminary and Yeshiva in Manchester. Current Jewish Student Chaplain based in Manchester serving over 2,000 Jewish Students. Author of the Book *Dancing Through Time*.

Rabbi Aubrey Hersh: Studied in Yeshivot in UK and Israel, after which he worked in media and advertising. Currently a senior lecturer at the JLE and Director of their Leadership Training Programme. Regular lecturer in various schools and United Synagogues, and a tour leader for trips to Eastern and Central Europe. aubrey@jle.org.uk

Rabbi Zvi Lieberman: Currently the Rabbi of Edgware Adath Yisroel Congregation. Involved in numerous rabbinical and educational activities in the fields of Kashrut. Acts as the Rabbinical Consultant to the Jewish Association for Business Ethics. rzhl@jabe.org

Rabbi Andrew Shaw: Graduated from Leeds University, with an engineering degree. Former National Education Director for UJS. Currently the assistant Rabbi of Stanmore United Synagogue and is the Executive Director of Tribe, Young United Synagogue. A regular *Muchni* lecturer.

Rabbi Steven Gaffin: Holds a degree in Psychology and also a Phd from London University. Currently the Executive Director of J-link an educational organisation which supports Jewish students in mainstream schools. rabbigaffin@jlink.org.uk

Rabbi Yaacov Haber: Rosh Yeshiva of Yeshivas Orchos Chaim in Jerusalem and President of TorahLab. yhaber@torahlab.org

Rabbi Danny Kirsch: Founder and Director of the JLE. Studied at various Yeshivot in Israel. Executive board member of Encounter.

Rabbi Gavin Broder: Former Chief Rabbi of Ireland, Rabbi of Newbury Park United Synagogue, Rabbi of Staines and District Synagogue. Currently the London Region Jewish Student Chaplain.

Rabbi Dr Julian Shindler: Director of the Marriage Authorisation Office for the Office of the Chief Rabbi. Currently the Executive Director of the Rabbinical Council of the United Synagogue. rabbi.shindler@chiefrabbi.org

Rabbi Michael Laitner: Assistant Rabbi at South Hampstead United Synagogue. Graduate of Yeshivat Hamivtar, the Sha'al Institute, and Leeds University.

Rabbi James Kennard: Educated at Oxford University. Former Jewish Student Chaplain based in Leeds. Currently the Head teacher of King Solomon High School in Essex.

Rabbi Chaim Rapoport: Former Minister in Birmingham and the Head of Birmingham Rabbinic Board. In 1997

assumed position as Rabbi to the Ilford United Synagogue, and was appointed as member of the Chief Rabbi's Cabinet holding the portfolio of Jewish Medical Ethics.

Rabbi Mordechai Ginsbury: Prinicpal of Hasmonean Primary School, Vice-Chairman, Rabbinical Council of the United Synagogue, former Rabbi of Prestwich Hebrew Congregation, Manchester. Currently the Rabbi of Hendon United Synagogue

Lieutenant Colonel Rabbi Jacob Goldstein: State Staff Chaplain of the New York Army National Guard. He has 18 military decorations and awards to his credit, including service in 1983 in Grenada, and Southwest Asia, and in the Middle East in 1991. He and his team participated in the rescue efforts at September 11. He also serves as Jewish Chaplain to the United States Secret Service.

Rabbi Ephraim Mirvis: Former Chief Rabbi of Ireland and Chairman of the Rabbinical Council of the United Synagogue. Currently the Rabbi of Finchley United Synagogue, Director of the Kinloss Learning Centre, Editor of Daf Hashavua, Religious Advisor to the Jewish Marriage Council. Member of the Chief Rabbi's Cabinet and the Standing Committee of the Conference of European Rabbis.

Esther Jungreis: Holocaust survivor, and Founder and President of Hineni, an international movement for Jewish people to return to their faith, has authored *Jewish Soul on Fire* and *A Committed Life*.

Tziporah Heller: International lecturer, faculty member of Neve Yerushalayim College in Jerusalem, specialises in Biblical literature, Jewish philosophy, Maimonides, the Maharal and the role of women in Judaism. Weekly columnist in Hamodia, and author of three books.

Rabbi Dr Shlomo Riskin: Internationally renowned educator, speaker and author. Founded and serves as Chancellor of Ohr Torah Stone Colleges and Graduate Programmes. He also serves as the founding Chief Rabbi of Efrat. Has published five books.

Rabbi Lawrence Kelemen: Professor of Education at Neve

Yerushalayim College in Jerusalem, regular lecturer at universities in medieval and modern Jewish philosophy.

Rabbi Yitzchak Reuven Rubin: Rabbi of Bowden Synagogue and Chairman of the Provincial Rabbinical Council. He is an author and columnist, and his interest in mental health led him to becoming elected the first Chairman of the Maimonides Hospital's outpatient facility.

Rivka Slonim: Educational Director at the Chabad House, Binghamton, New York. An internationally known teacher, lecturer, and activist. Author of "Total Immersion: A Mikveh Anthology."

Rabbi Herschel Billet: Studied at Yeshiva University. Currently the Rabbi of Young Israel of Woodmere. Elected President of the Rabbinical Council of America.

Rabbi Harvey Belovski: Oxford graduate with a degree in mathematics. Currently the Rabbi of Golders Green United Synagogue. Has broadcasted on BBC Radio, and is an author and lecturer. Regular teacher in the JLE Women's Programme and JLE Leadership Institute in London. rabbi@rabbibelovski.com

Rabbi Doron Kornbluth: Creator of the popular *Jewish Matters* pocketbook series, including *Jewish Matters* and *Jewish Women Speak*, and the author of *Why Marry Jewish?*

Sarah Robinson: A Jewish Studies teacher. Holds a Master's Degree in Hebrew and Jewish studies. She is a graduate of the Bradfield Scholar's Programme.

Rabbi Malcolm Herman: Graduate of Law. Programmes Director of seed UK which specialises in vibrant adult education.

Rabbi Richard Jacobs: Holds a degree in Zoology and worked for Jewish Student Chaplaincy and the Union of Jewish Students (UJS). Currently Director of Operations at the JLE. rjacobs@jle.org.uk

Zalman Noe: Born in Czechoslovakia. A prisoner in Auschwitz with the Sanz-Klausenberg Rebbe, who were both forced on the infamous Auschwitz death march. He currently lives in London with his wife and large family.

Rabbi Kalman Packousz: Executive Director of Aish Miami Beach, Florida. He was one of the first five students of Aish. Author of the 'Shabbat Shalom' fax.

Rabbi Saul Zneimer: Chief Executive of the United Synagogue. Previously the Rabbi of Kenton United Synagogue and Director of the Encounter Conference.

Sara Rigler: Graduate of Brandeis University. Her spiritual journey took her to India and through fifteen years of teaching Vedanta philosophy and meditation. Since 1987, she has been learning and teaching Torah, especially in Jerusalem's Old City, where she resides and writes.

Rabbi Daniel Rowe BA in philosophy from University College London. Former tank driver in the 401st Armoured Brigade of the IDF. Awarded an "Outstanding Soldier" award. Currently part of the Aish UK team.

Elie Wiesel: Born in Transylvania and a survivor of Auschwitz. A world famous author and playwright. Awarded the US Congressional Medal of Freedom in 1985 and the Nobel Prize for Peace in 1986.

Glossary

Abraham: The founder of Judaism and the physical and spiritual ancestor of the Jewish people. The first of the three Patriarchs of the Jewish People.

Adam: The first person God created. Lived in the Garden of Eden.

Agunot: A woman whose husband has refused her a religious divorce, which makes her bound in wedlock.

Al Kiddush Hashem: Sanctifying God's name.

Aliyah: Immigrating to Israel.

Amidah: (Silent Prayer) the central prayer in Judaism. It is recited 3 times a day and is made up of 19 blessings.

Aruch Hashulchan: A 19th Century work by Rav Yechiel Michel Epstein based on the *Shulchan Aruch*, analysing halachic issues.

Auschwitz: A Nazi extermination and concentration camp established in 1941 in south-western Poland.

Baal Shem Tov: 1700-1760. Rabbi Israel ben Eliezer, the founder of Chassidism.

Ba'al Teshuvah: A newly observant Jew.

Bar Mitzvah: A boy who has achieved the age of 13 and is consequently obligated to observe the commandments; also a ceremony marking the fact that a boy has achieved this age.

Bat Mitzvah: A girl who has achieved the age of 12 and is consequently obligated to observe the commandments; also a ceremony marking the fact that a girl has achieved this age.

BCE: Before the Common Era.

Beit HaMikdash: Holy Temple (twice destroyed) in Jerusalem.

Birkenau: The extermination camp 3km away from Auschwitz, which made up part of the Auschwitz-Birkenau concentration camp.

Brit Milah: The ritual circumcision of a male Jewish child on the 8th day of his life or of a male convert to Judaism.

Bubbe: Yiddish word for grandmother.

CE: In the Common Era.

Chafetz Chaim: 1840-1933. Considered one of the greatest leaders of his generation. Most famous for his commentary on the *Shulchan Aruch*, called the *Mishnah Brura*.

Chanukah: An eight-day festival celebrating the rededication of the Temple in Jerusalem after it was defiled by the Greeks.

Chanukiah: A eight-branched candelabra lit on *Chanukah*.

Chassidism (adj. Chassidic): Literally, "pious ones". Usually used in reference to a particular Orthodox movement founded by the *Baal Shem Tov* in Poland in the mid 18th century. There are various sects each of which follows their own *rebbe* as their leader.

Chazan: Cantor and leader of services in a synagogue.

Chessed: An act of kindness.

Chillul Hashem: Desecration of God's name. Causing God or Judaism to come into disrespect, or causing a person to violate a commandment.

Chuppah: The wedding canopy.

Chutzpah: Utter nerve; effrontery.

Dachau: Germany's first concentration camp, which opened in March 1933.

Dybuk (pl. Dybuks): In Jewish literature, the wandering soul of a dead person that enters the body of a living person and controls his or her behaviour.

Etrog: A citrus fruit used together with the *lulav* to fulfil the commandment of taking the four species, during the festival of *Succot*.

Garden of Eden: The garden of God and the first home of Adam and Eve.

Gemarah: Commentary on the *Mishnah*. The Mishnah and Gemarah together form the *Talmud*.

Genesis: First book of the *Torah*; known as Bereshit in Hebrew.

Golden Calf: Created and worshipped at the foot of *Mount Sinai* by the Jewish people.

Halachah (adj. Halachic): The complete body of rules and practices that Jews are bound to follow, including biblical commandments, commandments instituted by the Rabbis, and binding customs.

Haman: Formulated a plot to kill the Jewish Nation which forms the story of *Purim*.

Havdalah: A ritual marking the end of *Shabbat* or a festival.

Hillel: One of the greatest Rabbis recorded in the *Talmud*.

Holy of Holies: The inner sanctuary of the Temple, in which the Ark of the Covenant was kept.

Hy'd: abbreviation of 3 words 'Hashem yinakem damam' lit: may God avenge their blood. An appellation often used for Jewish martyrs.

Ibn Ezra: c.1089–1164. A Spanish grammarian, bible commentator, poet, philosopher and astronomer.

Isaiah: A Jewish prophet who lived at the time of the exile of the ten Tribes.

Kabbalah: Jewish mystical tradition.

Kapos: Inmates who supervised fellow prisoners in the Nazi Concentration Camps.

Kashrut: Jewish dietary laws.

Kedushah: Holiness.

King David: King of Israel. Author of Book of Psalms. Established Jerusalem as Israel's capital.

Kiddush: The prayer that is recited at the beginning of a festive meal on Shabbat and festivals, over a cup of wine.

Kiddush Ha-hayyim: Sanctification of life.

Kiddush Hashem: Sanctifying God's name.

Kippot (sing. Kippa): Head covering worn by Jewish men.

Kol Nidrei: The prayer service recited on the eve of *Yom Kippur*.

Kotel: The Western Wall of the Temple in Jerusalem.

Lulav: A collection of palm, myrtle and willow branches used together with the *etrog* to fulfil the commandment to "take the four species" during the festival of Succot.

Maccabees: A name for the family of heroes of the story of Chanukah, derived from the title of one of his sons, Judah the Maccabee.

Maggid of Mezeritch: Rabbi Dov Behr (d. 1772). The successor of the *Baal Shem Tov*, who organised *Chassidism* into a powerful movement.

Matzah (pl. Matzot): Unleavened bread eaten during *Pesach*.

Mentsch: A special person. One who can be respected for their moral behaviour.

Mezuzah (pl. Mezuzot): Biblical passage on a parchment scroll placed in a case and affixed to a doorpost.

Middot: (Virtuous) character traits.

Midrash: Stories elaborating on incidents in the Bible, to derive a principle of Jewish law or provide a moral lesson.

Mikveh: A special pool of water, used for the purpose of attaining ritual purity.

Minyan: The quorum necessary to recite certain prayers, consisting of ten adult Jewish men.

Mir: One of the biggest and most famous of all Yeshivot with over 2,000 students.

Mishkan: Holy Temple used by the Children of Israel in the wilderness.

Mishnah: A written compilation of the oral tradition (c.200CE), the basis of the *Talmud*.

Mitzvah (pl. Mitzvot): Any of the 613 commandments that Jews are obligated to observe; it can also refer to any Jewish religious obligation, or more generally to any good deed.

Mordechai: The hero in the Purim story, who thwarted Haman and saved the Jewish people.

Moses: The person who led the Jewish People out of exile in Egypt, through the desert to Mount Sinai where they received the Torah. The greatest of all Jewish prophets.

Moshiach: The man who will be chosen by God to end all evil in the world, rebuild the Temple and usher in the World to Come.

Mount Sinai: The mountain at which the Jewish People received the Torah.

Muchni: A mechanism designed to lower the laver into contact with the water table. A term used to describe an in-depth educational talk.

Neilah: The closing service of *Yom Kippur*.

Neshamah: The soul.

Niddut: The separation of a woman from her husband during her menstrual period.

Ohr HaChayim: 1696-1743. Rabbi Chaim ben Atar. His saintly way of life gained him the name Ohr HaChayim HaKadosh (the holy one).

Olam Ha'ba: The World to Come.

Onkelos: A convert to Judaism who provided a renowned aramaic commentary on the Torah.

Oral Law: Jewish teachings explaining and elaborating on the Written Torah, handed down orally until the 2nd century CE, when they began to be written down in what became the Talmud.

Patriarchs: Abraham, Isaac and Jacob.

Payot: (Lit. corners) Colloquially, ringlets. A response to the law of not cutting an area of hair around the ear. Many different customs stem from this depending on the community.

Pesach: A festival commemorating the Exodus from Egypt; also known as Passover.

Pikuach Nefesh: The principle of being allowed to violate Jewish law to save a life.

Pshat: The basic understanding of a concept or idea.

Purim: A holiday celebrating the rescue of the Jews from extermination at the hands of the chief minister to the King of Persia (4th century BCE) as related in the Book of Esther.

Rabbi Akiva: One of the greatest Rabbis recorded in the Talmud. Died a martyr for the Jewish People c.135CE.

Rabbi JB Soloveitchik: 1903-1993. Rosh Yeshiva of Yeshiva University and prolific orator and author. Father figure of Modern Orthodoxy in the United States.

Rabbi Yehudah Halevi: c.1080 – 1145. A Spanish Talmudic scholar known for his philosophy and poetry.

Rabbi Yehudah HaNasi: Lived in 2nd century CE and compiled the *Mishnah*. He is also known as Rebbi throughout the *Mishnah*.

Rabbi Yochanan (ben Zakai): Leader of the Jewish people at the time of the destruction of the *Second Temple*.

Rambam: 1135-1204. Rabbi Moshe ben Maimon. One of the greatest medieval Jewish scholars. Also known as Maimonides and renowned for his codification of Jewish Law and his Guide to the Perplexed.

Rashi: 1040-1105. Rabbi Shlomo Yitzchaki. The most famous Jewish Commentator who wrote on the entire *Torah* and *Talmud*.

Rav: Term of endearment for Rabbi.

Rebbe: Means Grand Rabbi. This person is the leader of a *Chassidic* community, often believed to have special, mystical power.

Rosh Chodesh: The beginning of every Jewish month.

Rosh Hashanah: The Jewish new year.

Rosh Yeshiva: The spiritual head of a Yeshiva.

Saadia Gaon: Lived c.882 – 942 CE. Leader of Jewry and author of major philosophical work.

Sarah: Was married to Abraham. One of the four Matriarchs.

Schlepp: A Yiddish word to drag, carry or haul.

Second Temple: Built in Jerusalem (c.350BCE-70CE)

Sefer HaChinuch: A comprehensive description of the 613 commandments, arranged according to their appearance in the Torah, written in 13th century Spain.

Sefer Torah: A Torah scroll.

Shabbat: The Jewish Sabbath.

Shechitah: Religious slaughter of animals.

Shekel: The currency of Israel. The main silver coin in Biblical and Temple times.

Shema: One of the fundamental Jewish prayers, taken from verses in the Torah.

Shivah: Seven day period for family and close relatives of the deceased, in order to mourn their loved one.

Shoah: The Holocaust.

Shofar: A ram's horn blown on Rosh Hashanah like a trumpet as a call to repentance.

Shtetl: A small Jewish town or village formerly found throughout Eastern Europe.

Shulchan Aruch: A code of Jewish law written by Rabbi

Joseph Caro in the 16th century, and one of the most respected and important compilations ever written.

Siddur: Prayer book.

Simcha: Joy. Also used to describe a happy occasion.

Succah: The temporary dwellings lived in during the festival of *Succot*.

Succot: A festival commemorating God's protection in the wilderness and also the final harvest; also known as the Feast of Tabernacles or the Festival of Ingathering.

Taharat Hamishpacha: Laws relating to the separation of husband and wife during the woman's menstrual period.

Talmud (Babylonian): The most significant collection of the Jewish oral tradition interpreting the Torah (late 5th century CE).

Talmud (Jerusalem): A companion to the Babylonian Talmud but written in Israel 150 years earlier (4th century CE).

Techiyat HaMetim: Revival or resurrection of the dead and one of the fundamental beliefs of the Jewish Religion.

Tefillin: Biblical passages on parchment scrolls placed in small leather boxes and affixed with leather straps; worn during morning prayer by adult men.

Tehillim: The Book of Psalms.

Tenach: The written Bible. Referred to as the 'Old Testament' by non-Jews.

Theresienstadt: A concentration camp located 35 miles from Prague. As the war progressed Theresienstadt became a transit camp for Jews bound for *Auschwitz*.

Tisha B'Av: The 9th day of the Jewish month Av. The destruction of both Temples, as well as much other Jewish suffering, happened on this day throughout history.

Torah: In its narrowest sense, the first five books of the Bible: Genesis, Exodus, Leviticus, Numbers and Deuteronomy, sometimes called the Pentateuch; in its broadest sense, Torah is the entire body of Jewish teachings.

Tower of Babel: A tower built by Noah's descendants (probably in Babylon) who intended it to reach up to heaven; God foiled them by confusing their language so they could no longer understand one another (Genesis Chapter 11).

Tumah: Ritual impurity.

Tzedakah: Lit. righteousness. Generally refers to charity.

Tzaddikim: (sing. Tzaddik) Righteous people.

Tzitzit: Specially knotted fringes worn by men on their four-cornered garments.

Yeshiva (pl. Yeshivot): An academy of religious study for men.

Yizkor: Memorial service held on certain holidays in honour of deceased relatives and members of the Community.

Yom Kippur: The Day of Atonement; a day set aside for fasting and repenting from the sins of the previous year.

Zeida: Yiddish word for grandfather.